THE WONDER OF IT ALL

Earl Fee

Order this book online at www.trafford.com
or email orders@trafford.com

Most Trafford titles are also available at major online book retailers.

Printed in the United States of America.

ISBN: 978-1-4669-7589-7 (sc)
ISBN: 978-1-4669-7588-0 (e)

Trafford rev. 01/18/2013

www.trafford.com

North America & international
toll-free: 1 888 232 4444 (USA & Canada)
phone: 250 383 6864 • fax: 812 355 4082

INTRODUCTION

"Poetry reveals to us the loveliness of nature, brings back the freshness of youthful feelings, reviews the relish of simple pleasures, keeps unquenched the enthusiasm which warmed the spring time of our being, refines youthful love, strengthens our interest in human nature, by vivid delineations of its tenderest and softest feeling and through the brightness of its prophetic visions, helps faith [and hope] to lay hold on the future life."
William Ellery Channing

The above quotation is a good summary of the major advantages of reading and enjoying poetry. But I believe there is another important advantage—namely poetry can increase your spirituality by awakening the senses of taste, sight, hearing, and heart feelings. The aspect of spirituality I speak of is defined here as your loving, kind, compassionate actions in dealing with your fellow man, helping others, and making the world a better place by sharing your gifts with the world. It's a feeling of benevolent identification with nature, all mankind and all forms of life. When you are more aware and appreciative of everything around you—your appreciation of nature increases, your empathy for your fellow man increases and your spirituality grows. This in turn leads to a greater quality of life. As one gets older spirituality can increase, but the mind and body deteriorate. There is a feeling that time is running out,—so each hour becomes more precious.

Poetry will help sharpen your sensory skills so that you are more aware of sights, even subtle sounds and aromas, and more attune to feelings of others. Aim to be enjoy each precious hour to the fullest extent. Aim to be like a Dr. Zhivago, the poet/physician/ lover in the great movie of the same name. He was constantly aware and appreciative of his surroundings. But most people are not smelling the roses. They are seeing but not really seeing and appreciating. They are wearing blinkers. It's like hearing but not listening to your spouse. A good example of wearing the blinkers was In the Globe and Mail recently, where: a writer extols the advantages of living in the far north in Canada. She mentioned the crisp air, the great meals at the neighbours and the spring flowers, but no mention of the Northern lights, sunsets and sunrises, the beautiful surroundings, the different sounds or silence, or the awesome and plentiful stars that are missing in our cities due to smog and glare.

Take off the blinkers. By greater appreciation of nature and your fellow man you become a poet yourself. George Sand states: *"He who draws delights from the sentiment of poetry is a true poet, though he has never even written a line in all his life."*

Finally, you may wonder why the title; The Wonder of It All? Any day that we do not hear the voices of our 14 billion year old still evolving universe: revel in a vibrant golden sunrise or a soul stirring sunset, the magic clouds and a clear blue sky, or an awesome starry night; appreciate a walk in nature, or appreciate our fellow man and creatures; is a wasted day. Our lives are too outwardly materialistically oriented, whereas they should be more inwardly spiritually sensitive.

In my city I sadly miss the nightly display of our universe. In the county this spectacle so available each night in the crisp clear air—is normally taken for granted. We need to be more appreciative of the 100 billion galaxies and roughly 100 billion stars in each galaxy and with some stars so monstrous that it would take a jet plane about 1100 years to travel around them. Hence, it is impossible that we are alone in the universe. Recent research by astronomers reveals the universe is no doubt teeming with trillions of worlds like our own. We need to be forever grateful to be a finite part of our infinite, mind boggling, universe that defies description. Therefore, hopefully these few words will be food for thought—and these meager offerings of poems and impressive professional photos will awaken some spiritual appreciation and gratitude for the wonder of it all.

ACKNOWLEDGEMENTS

I give thanks to my good friend Wayne Cosgrove, poet, who started me on my poetry writing in the 1990's by inviting me to his poetry parties where everyone had to bring their meagre offerings. One of my poems, The Flower Lady in the Oasis, was inspired by his own fine poem on this subject—and another one was inspired by one of his personal quotations: "Lovers come and go, but friendship goes on forever."

The many professional photos used from Canstockphoto, and a few from iStockphoto including the great cover photo are gratefully acknowledged.

The action photo of me in the 200 meter hurdles—a world record in Puerto Rico, September 2010 at age 81—by professional photographer Francesco "Paquito" Lopez" is gratefully acknowledged. See poem Old Suckers Never Stop in the Laugh section.

Used here are two impressive expressionist paintings in acrylic—painted by my late brother Maurice Fee. These and over 130 others were bequeathed to me. The two here are, the Laugh title page (The Clown), and in the Live section with the poem Faces (Melancholy). As always I am greatly appreciative of these remarkable paintings making me feel grateful and wealthy.

CONTENTS

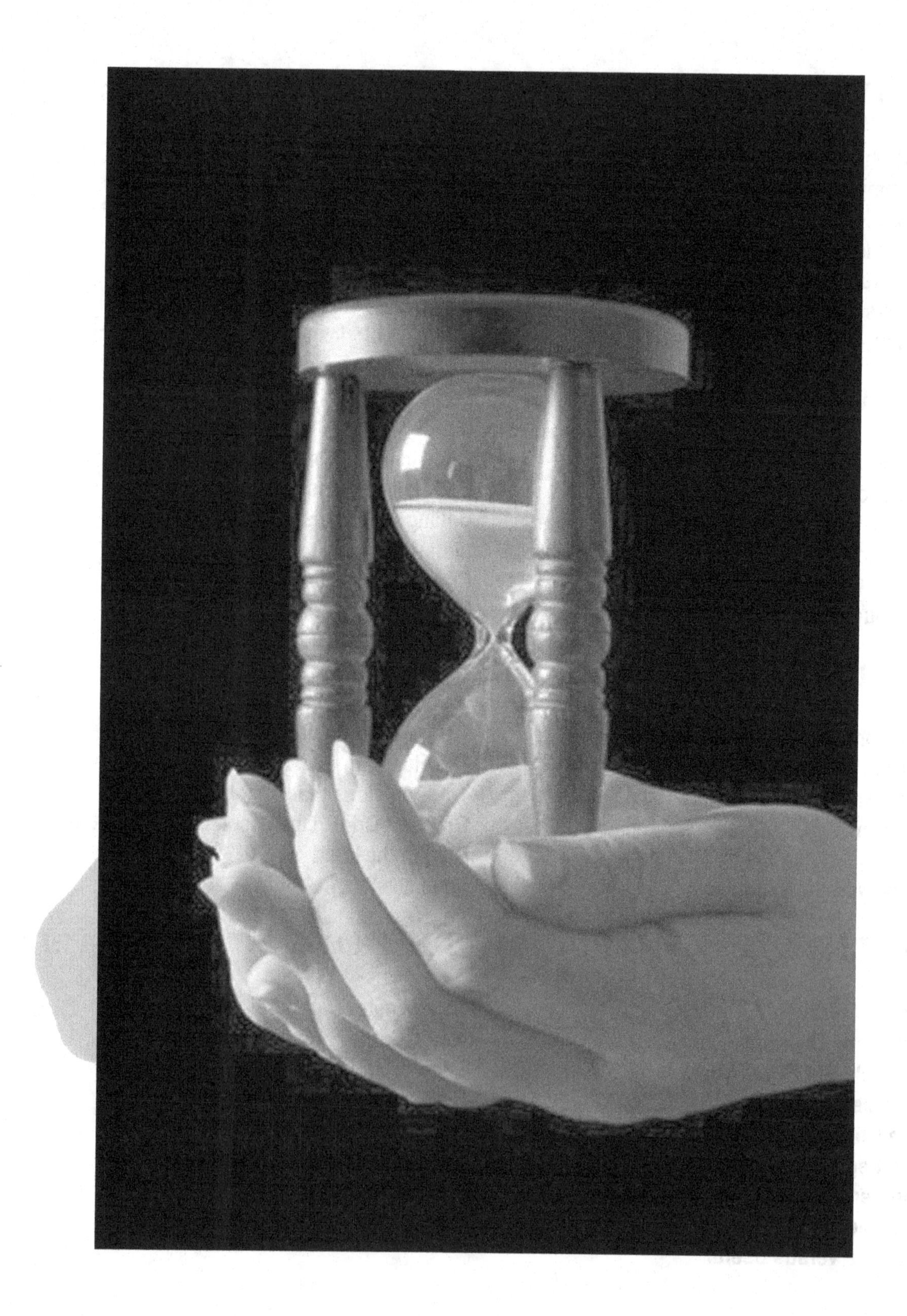

LIVE

The Trilliums

It's early May and heaven on earth
It seems, as I tread the forest path
So still and fresh. My heart is filled with mirth
For in spring how could one have wrath?
Beside me a stream shines and whispers;
While on the forest floor an ocean
Of white trilliums perform their vespers
With velvet throats raised in devotion,
To sing silent amens one and all
To their deceased neighbours the brown leaves;
Above, silver columns form nature's cathedral
With a new roof of green and lacy weaves.
To make my day complete a cardinal
In suit of blazing red comes to greet
"Farewell! Come again!" I know I shall,
As refreshed I emerge to the hot street.
But will the trilliums still be there?
In life there are too many farewells I swear.

Drifting Clouds

White drifting clouds slowly traverse the sky,
Blessed by the golden sun smiling on high,
Likewise our sorrows will take flight and fly
To another world to disappear and die.

Fleeting Dreams

Your dreams are in the sky
Like bright clouds drifting by;
Latch onto one—catch a ride—
Time's a wasting—no time to bide.

Buried Dreams

Many a golden dream sweated on for years
Languishes—abandoned—
In the dark archives of the mind.
Never to see glorious light of day.
The cobwebs of time overcomes all;
Will you dream be so?
Or will it see the enlightening dawn of day?

Second Chances

They asked what is the best time of the day?
I did not have to think:
"The dawn of a new day:
Born again—
In the rays of the new born sun—
Bringing promise of a fresh start;
Adventure, intrigue and love.
It's all in the eager air.
Born again—
To chase our dreams;
To start a new dream;
To make amends for yesterdays;
To forget past trials;
And to love again."

Erected
Society
Toronto

Mount Pleasant Cemetery

Those rushing happily by will suffer similar fates
As the near two-hundred-thousand within these iron gates.
For one hundred and twenty years they came one by one;
Oft'times with sweat and pick and shovel their graves were done.

Oh—its tranquil beauty and gardens are beyond compare
For those left behind to reminisce and their sorrow share.
A place for freeing souls—Mount Pleasant Cemetery;
If I must be buried, 'tis there I wish to tarry.

A place for all nationalities for a moment
In infinite time; where a tree can be a monument;
Where sundials, and hundred-year-old pioneer trees abound;
Where markers grandiose, simple, or odd, do not astound.

On symbolic memorials unending see the lily,
Cross and crown, laurel, clover, Celtic cross and ivy,
Beautiful Greek columns, olive branch, the hand of God,
Pagoda rooftops, and Fu Chu dogs looking so odd.

Here you will find the not so famous like Stephen Oliver,
But many famous: Glenn Gould, Charlie Conacher,
Timothy Eaton, Charles Best and Frederick Banting,
Foster Hewitt, and William Lyon Mackenzie King.

Come walk in hand with me as golden shafts of sunlight dance
On trees of all species and myriad coloured plants;
Now move into the cool shaded aisles where one could get lost
Since a multitude of straight and winding paths are crossed.

Near the gates off Yonge Street lies football star Johnny Copp
By a spreading chestnut tree and traffic that will not stop;
In nineteen-thirty-three this young hero at U of T
Was shot—gunned down by an enemy he did not see.

When the mighty Empress of Ireland slipped Quebec City
God had planned a fateful frigid meeting without pity.
The 'Saly Ann' played "God Be With You Till We Meet Again"
But over one-thousand would never again hear that strain.

In the fog a sinister mate the collier Storsted
Drew too near then collided—littering the river with dead.
Promoted to glory forever says the monument lists
For one-hundred and sixty-seven lost Salvationists.

Approach the historic mausoleum with trepidation;
Outside two copper beech trees are stunning in the sun;
Inside rests Canada's greatest War One pilot hero
Colonel Barker; to fifty enemy planes he brought woe.

The sky was filled with rose petals from six aircraft en route
Over the mausoleum and chapel to pay tribute;
And to honour his skill, courage, Victoria Cross,
Distinguished Service Order, and Military Cross.

See in his cold marble crypt an angel, on stained window,
With wide brown wings, and this stirring inscription below:

"His love shall beacon you through the night
And lead you upward into radiant day;
Within the shelter of his brooding wings,
Your parting spirit shall find sweet repose."

Flight 621 is forever remembered here where squirrel
And chipmunk scamper; over one-hundred were at peril
When outboard engine of the 'Galaxy' fell at lift-off.
The stone immense bears inscriptions of all lives cut-off.

Families of three, four, and five gone with scarce time to pray,
Like Weinberg, Whittingham, Wong, Benson, and Belanger
On July five, nineteen-seventy when in their prime;
Now they lie beside a huge catalpa withered by time.

The proud Lusitania was sent to the dreary deep
In nineteen-fifteen by a German sub that did creep
With sleek grey stealth—silently off the coast of Ireland;
And two-thousand souls were sent to another land,

With corpses resting where fishes darted and sea worms stirred;
Ninety-eight from Toronto were icily interred;
Martha Waites was one of them now in 76 section.
We pray they shall receive His glorious benediction.

There are countless sad and happy memories recalled here;
The monuments stand guard and stand the wear of time each year
And all too often outliving the precious memories;
One wonders are some gone—watching with sadness and unease.

Here in this bird paradise, pain is eased by God's beauty;
Pray let us not forget our departed and our duty
Here where souls are set free, in Mount Pleasant Cimetiere.
If we shall be buried—let it be there—let it be there.

The Danger of Deprecating the Disadvantaged

Many a time as a young lad in Toronto the Good
I witnessed Uncle Wellwood—
a butcher of cattle in Detroit—
Simulating his wooden-leg jig,
With a skip and a slap-happy hop . . .,
Always after too much of the snake-bite poison
On many a joyous family get-together.
A decade or so later, he lost a big toe from gangrene . . .
Then the lower foot . . .
And eventually the whole lower leg above the knee.
Strange that it should happen to him.
Then he could have danced
a most realistic wooden-leg jig,
But no! The fun of it, like his limb were both lost.
Was this payback time?
Six decades later I still often wonder.

Not Yet Lord

God gently beckoned him;
The offer was there.
Too often life is not fair,
But Death is all too grim,
So he said, "Not now Lord."

One must sink or swim;
Those who sink, sink fast;
Those who swim, they last.
Living is more than a whim,
So he said, "Later Lord."

If only there was more time.
He thought of wasted years
And of needless tears
He'd caused in selfish clime,
So he said, "Not yet Lord."

Now he could clearly see
How to make amends
To neglected friends,
Loved ones and family,
So he said, "Not today Lord."

When life is drifting away—
Life seems all too priceless;
All else is senseless
Next to earthly living,
So he said, "Not yet Lord."

Night Storm

The dark heavens were seething with a cacophony of sound and fury, boiling over with anger, revolting against the afternoon peace of the fiery heat. My roof resounded as if a thousand hammers were pounding on a thousand anvils. I sprang from my bed to the window to witness the sky in turmoil. The heavens were venting its infinite energy in billions of tons of rain pounding, hammering the earth; with thousands of blinding lightning bolts flung down to Earth as if in punishment, but for what crime? Bolt upon silver jagged bolt piercing the blackness. A thousand oceans were roaring. A thousand giant Gods were blowing, lashing, thrashing Mother Nature. Giant white stallions with thunderous hoofs pounding, and roaring lions with enormous tails thrashing, were charging against each other, charging across the heavens back-and-forth, back-and-forth. Some were pulling gigantic chariots which rattled and clattered across the sky. Their mysterious black riders threw lightning bolts as they sped by at the speed of light . . .

And then—all sped a million miles away to another world, taking the turmoil with them. I was left only with the soft patter of gentle rain like falling dewdrops on my shingles and my now serene garden and soft lawn, and the murmur of a storm turning into a whisper, and a distant flickering light . . .

I returned to my safe warm bed with an immense impression of the power of the Almighty, and smiling within to have lived this experience, and forever grateful to be a finite part of this infinite universe.

God Has Smiled On You Today

Sometimes you strike a rare golden day:
It's a great-to-be-alive day;
You feel like the lottery came in;
Your spirits soar;
You know this is one of the happiest days
of your life;
Some ecstatic joyful hormones have arrived;
No particular reason.
Perhaps the sun is in its glory,
A golden sunset a sunrise,
Or the snow is glistening with a billlion stars,
Or a warm spring rain is softly falling,
Or the night has hung out a trillion
white lanterns.
But it is not so much the season or the climate,
It's just one of those days.
All is positive,
Could occur any time,
Rare and glorious euphoria.
Then you are a millionaire
In friends, family, health, glory and success.
Something turned you on,
But in your heart you glow.
And it is hard to say
Why God has smiled on you today.

Last Drink With Grandad

The stroke had laid him low—
Now on an ambulance bed,
In the cottage perched high over Eagle Lake,
He must have known his time was
drawing near—
And we all knew.
How he loved the apricot brandy—
We shared one together—me standing
by his side.
I was his favorite grandson
And he was the greatest, the strongest,
And also the best reciter of Robert Service
poems,
But only after a drink or two.
Sixty years ago I used to think:
When I grow up I want to be like Grandad.
Grandma was a dear, loveable person too,
Walking tall, gracing the world with
her presence,
And only a kind word about everyone.
And after forty years of hard work
Amid the golden wheat fields
Near Saskatoon Saskatchewan
And sixty years of love,
She knew well his likes and dislikes.
So I shared one last drink with Grandad.

A Special Friend

In this brief lifetime
We are truly blessed
And fortunate beyond compare
If we have a special friend who:
Cultivates the friendship through the years;
Not allowing the weeds to grow;
Alleviates our worst fears;
Is there when needed without urging;
Gives without receiving;
Understands and asks not;
Says what you need to hear;
Forgives and tolerates our weaknesses;
And truly cares.
With such a friend you are rich indeed
though poor.
I have found a treasure it's true
For such a one is you,
Dear friend!

A Retirees Prayer of Survival

The night throws on a grey veil over the sun
And finally puts on its cloak of infinite stars.
I pray Lord make it swift,
this black nothingness called sleep.
Time is a wasting, let us fly through it
To the beginning of flickering light
And on to the Dance of Life:
The hustle and bustle of satisfaction
of mind, body and soul.
Unfortunately for most it's satisfaction of
body only.
Forgive them.
And if perchance dreams may come—
Let them be useful, loving and intuitive,
Rather than the usual meaningless wanderings
of weird characters and unbelievable actions.
Oh yes Lord! lead us not to the Big Sleep,
Just the usual fitful one.

A Whale of a Home

The home of a friend in Oregon, USA west coast

Ah peacefulness—to witness from on high
The ever rolling waves beyond the tranquil bay.
Almost every hour a new view brings a sigh;
At morn the quiet time, at noon the silver spray
And perchance to watch the awesome whales at play.
At cloak of night blessed is the crimson sunset
And the moon shining where waters softly snore.
But now it's daybreak and how can one forget:
To revel in God's work just beyond the door;
To slowly walk by sculptured cliffs where spirits soar—
Like an eagle observing the vast expanse—
Of ocean kingdom for miles and miles around;
And then to stroll in summer heat mid cool green plants.
Now I see, where such beauty and peace abound,
There can be no desire or dream to stray or roam
And it's possible to have heaven in a home.

Advice to a Son and Daughter

You are a grown man and woman now;
There should have been more advice,
For love is not enough.
But I tried to set a good example
And instil kind thoughts in you.
Firstly, there is a God—you can't see Him,
But He's there;
Our minds are too tiny to grasp infinity;
Sometimes you feel Him working:
In the goodness in other's hearts,
In the fresh spring air,
In the tiny glistening snowflake,
In the galaxy of white stars on a still night
Holding sovereignty over all.
Sometimes you will wonder
When you encounter evil in the world,
But God works in wondrous ways.
And there is an archangel somewhere
within us all.
The best advice I can give you
Is live the Christian way;
Be one who keeps their word;
Be a helper and kindness
Will be returned in the long haul.
There will be times:
When you must be as strong as steel,
And when you must be soft and caring;
Hopefully these will come naturally
Without feigning or acting.
So strive to be sincere in your dealings
With your fellow man;
Always count your blessings;
Your real riches are your loved ones
And your health;
Remember you will have the body and face
You deserve when you are eighty
So look after them
While maintaining your sense of humor.

Be well advised that the world turns
On a gigantic pivot of gold—money!
And floats on a magic carpet of dollar bills;
Our lives roll along on billions of coin.
All this can fly away in a moment of madness
Taking years to replace,
And there are evil ones to wrest it from you,
Even kill for it in a twinkling.
So do not be too trusting;
Beware of the deal too good,
And the talkers too smooth;
Make no deal or big decision
When the nerves are jangling,
This is your subconscious

Telling you of its vast buried experience;
So listen intently to your intuition;
That mistake made in haste
Against the advice of friends
Can haunt you and burn your soul,
Like a giant vulture on your shoulder,
Constantly picking away at your brain,
And cause a fire in your belly
Like a red hot poker that will not leave.
But if knocked down—by misfortune—
Then is the time to get up,
Although bloodied and perhaps disgraced
Rising higher than before.

Oh Blasted Wind

A storm on the shores of Lake Huron, Ontario

When the mighty lake does gently wash and wash,
I like it fine—I'm lifted to exotic shores;
And when the mirror waters are bound to silence,
It's most divine—my mind is soothed in tranquil balm.
But, when the great rollers roar and roar
And roar some more with their crash on crash on crash;
All the winds of the world direct on my rocky shore;
Sending the forest into revolting fury
And shaking and whistling through my humble retreat:
Like twenty freight locomotives passing,
Or fifty motorcycles revving and revving,
Or one-hundred wonky lawn mowers churning,
Or two-hundred wronged women wailing,
All through the infinite night—then I say no more.
I pack my bags, and say you win, oh blasted wind
As I hastily blow town.

The Last Toot

The brass French horn lay silent for many
a year
Lost to the world,
In the attic dust with only a spider
And it's web for companions;
Destined never to shine or speak again.
If it could speak what tales would it unfold?
What hands and lips wrought its tune?
What revelry would it recall?
With forlorn call—
Reverberating through dark woods
And over misty hill and dale,
What danger did it warn?
Did it reside in peaceful pastoral home?
And on occasion raise the hounds to beck
and call?
Or abide in bustle of city smog,
And sometimes grace the ear in grand orchestra
or mighty band?

But then one sunny day for dollars five
it was mine,
And freed from its dark prison.
Now it would sing and glisten again
And long after we are gone.
The horn's past master blew one last blast,
"That's the last toot for me," said he.

So live for the day
For we know not when the last hurrah
Suddenly will come,
Never more to love again,
To feel the soft rain of spring,
To feel the warm sun on skin,
To marvel at the silent sleeping stars,
To feel love accelerate in fond embrace,
To hear, to see, to feel, God's handiwork
Never more.
It's all just a fleeting memory—
Like a happy yet sad note drifting lonely from
a horn—
When He decides you've had—
That last toot.

Last Ride to Somewhere

When you're a teenager
You're oblivious to the hearse
Passing by . . .
By middle age, it might catch your eye.
As a senior, you're driving the school bus
Or even the hearse.
A decade later you're a passenger
Riding in the hearse
On the road to Somewhere
Or for some to Nowhere.
While most ignore thoughts of this curse—
The wise man knows how to:
Delay—delay—delay—
To stay your ride to Wherever.
The secret is the healthy way
Decades before our bonds do sever.

Vietnam Serenade

In a bunker in steamy Vietnam
In the blackness a GI played his harmonica
Softly, longingly.
A foolish brave thing to do;
His eyes darted to and fro;
His sixteen ever ready;
Eyes cocked for any surreptitious movement
On the other side of a silver strand of river
Blessed by the full moon.
Over there under sixty-foot tall trees
lurked the Vietcong:
Some alert, some lulled by the notes drifting
In the slow rush of the hot humid wind.
As he played he mused
That's the same moon over my home
Over two thousand miles away.
Behind him his mates each in a man-made nest
Absorbed each floating note,
Each soothing note,
Knowing there was safety except perhaps
When the music stopped.
He played on—disobeying his colonel—
Didn't give a damn.
Tonight in the moonlight killing time—
Tomorrow in the dawn, killing "gooks."

JULY
IV

Date in New York City

Saturday night in New York City.
Leave the graffiti an' screechin' subway behind,
Stride into the neon night
Feelin' high, feelin' high as a 'scraper.
The neon lights are 'lectricity
Runnin' up and down my spine
Pulsin' in my veins.
The clangin', an' blarin', is racin'
In my heart.
Move shoes, move crowd!
Love the rush, the bustle
Like a mechanical jungle,
The traffic roarin' like a thousand lions.
New York, I been here two years,
But seems like twenty,
Packed in a lot of livin',
Love it when it's singin' and dancin',
Love it when it's 'sleepin'.
Move shoes, 'scuse me crowd!
She'll be waitin' under the big sign,
The orange, the green, the blue and the flashin' red.
I can smell her perfume now,
Heavy but sweet.
Grab a cab to our club,
The gang will be there
In the smoke, the laughter,
Love that banjo, honky tonk piano, the sax,
And the cold beer.
Move shoes, pardon crowd!
Too soon the city will put on its dark cloak,
Its giant breast is heavin' softly now.
In the morn my gal will be in my arms,
But how do you embrace a city?
Love em both!
We'll awake to yellow shafts of sunlight
Through the basement window,
Smellin' the aroma of fresh coffee.
Damnit! woke up by that truck
washin' the streets agin'.
Then the awakenin' of an ocean of cars,
Wave upon wave,
An' this time like the purrin' of a thousand kittens.
The giant is awake and stompin' slow.
Later a walk in the park:
Giant trees, fast and also lazy runners,
pesky and frisky dogs.
Stop at our favorite, the Alice and Wonderland statue,
Drink in the wonderment of it all.
New York you are a wonder!
Move shoes, step aside crowd—
I see her now,
It's time for livin', and lovin', once agin'.

The Fisherman and His Last Catch

Inspired by a painting by Winslow Homer
from the Boston Art Gallery.

The high seas are roaring,
the spray cold to the bone;
the wind is speaking loud now,
and my arms are dead from rowing, rowing.
Pull on, pull on.
Black storm rollin' in and darkness;
Don't like the looks of it.
Been out for six hours
and only two big fish;
what a job to get them in;
the captain will be disappointed.
Pull on, pull on.
My bunk and mates and some warm grog
look a long way off,
perhaps a mile,
with all sails up,
and pulling away with the wind.
In these high caps will they see me,
or lose me in the approaching blackness?
Pull on, pull on.
Light is dying fast;

Ominous clouds moving in rapidly now.
The ship is not in sight.
Why did I return for one last sail?
How I miss my Susan and the wee ones,
in that cottage by the sea.
Will I see them again?
My mates will not forsake me,
but it's the last catch for me
for my body says no more.
Pull on pull on,
But which direction?

The Last Lap

Speed beckoned where only he would dare,
Then the Ferrari twirled in the air . . .
To disintegrate while thousands stare;
Doing the thing he loved to do;
One last time while to his demise he flew.

Misery Likes Company

The pain was beyond belief.
When my friend phoned to complain—
Happy was I to share my pain.
When he said he had it too—
I was better and no longer blue.

The Karate Chop

Two inches of solid pine was fine,
He'd break it without whimper or whine.
Then the day of the hysterical joke:
His broken hand told it was knotted oak.

Fraternity

This war, this Hell forged our fraternity;
"He'd do it for me"—our philosophy.
There was Jim, George and Mac, the big three,
But in the end—pity—there was only me.

Work, Work, Work as a Boy

On Grandad's farm as a tiny tot
I first earned pennies and cherished my lot:
Catching gophers at one cent per tail,
And piling sheaves of wheat one cent per bail.

Work, work, work started for me at eight,
A task my brother and I did hate;
Selling mother's donuts door to door;
Days of poverty to deplore.

Shovelling snow when blizzards blow,
When it piled high it was time to go,
But if the reward was too slim—
We shovelled it back ag'in with vim.

Navigator for my blind cousin:
Lake Gravenhurst was his picture within;
We toured the islands—I was his eyes,
But getting lost on several tries.

Selling papers was not much joy:
I lacked the drive as a shy young boy.
Dropping flyers for a buck or two;
Forgive me Lord I did dump a few.

Delivering groceries on my bike
To sexy ladies, but alas still a tyke.
Then rats I had to drown at night;
The welcome pay didn't make it right.

At Barker's bakery sorting garbage,
Then on to baking at meagre wage.
I remember still the sad day we
Left out the sugar in tons of cookie.

Then when older at CN freight shed
Loading dynamite, and coffins with dread,
Barrels of chains, tons of coffee and tea.
A mystery who stole those "cigs"—not me.

At the "Ex"[Toronto Exhibition], brother and
I were grand:
We scalped tickets to the Grandstand.
In this service we tried to be fair,
But "A" seats were the worst—buyer beware.

During the Second World War I toiled
In munitions where my mind got soiled.
On day a General came up to me,
"It helps to know the answer," said he.

A miracle I survived there at all:
One day a machine took off my overall,
Next a grinder burst—but missed my seat,
Later a ton of steel fell at my feet.

As a draftsman at Ideal Stoker,
At sixteen, I only once did err.
Fifty cents an hour for many a design,
But let's face it, I was no Einstein.

Hard to say how these jobs shaped a boy;
Difficult to say they were a joy.
The pennies earned were spent quite soon,
But the memories remain for many a moon.

The Iditarod

Now their time was nigh with his dogs in a frenzy,
Straining at the traces, yapping and spinning,
While thirty dog teams had burst out explosively;
All eager to start the thousand miles of running.

He lifted the snow hook with a lightning, "Let's go!"
The sled shot forward as a spring uncoiled—
And was nearly airborne in spite of scarce snow;
And never had his nine friends so joyfully toiled.

Now straining every sinew in the harness;
They knew not how far or how treacherous the trail,
So they knew not fear and longed not for largesse;
Their reward was but to strive with no thought to fail.

Now with the energy eruption and crowds behind,
As the sled and each mile slipped by—confident was he;
For such loyalty and bond with his team was rare to find.
Now they strived to prove they would be all they could be.

Only their master knew of the pitfalls ahead:
The surprises that could befall between twenty check points;
Delirium—falling asleep behind the sled;
The body a mass of aching muscles and joints;

To feel the Alaska Monster of wind and snow
With its breath oft'times of twenty or thirty knot,
Or its hoary breath of a minus sixty below,
While mushing twenty hours per day for a prize each sought;

Then the days of soaring heat—too torrid to help push his team;
With reluctant sled creeping slow over sticky snow;
And through dazed eyes to watch as in a fiery dream,
Dogs panting and straining but still eager to go.

Hallucinating through half closed eyes that tire:
"How far ahead is Joe? I must make up an hour—
Let's fly! come on boys we can set this trail on fire—
We've got one spare tire left—no need to cower."

Now stopping! and dreaming into the midnight twilight,
Then up at four a.m. in the eerie silence of dawn;
The headlamps bobbing through thick woods and waining starlight;
This is not for the weak and timid—this marathon;

For one could meet a mad bull moose on the trail;
Or make a wrong turn—the leader is not always right;
Yes, so easy to give in, so easy to fail
In the nine to eighteen days before Nome swings in sight.

Scarce time is there to stare at Alaska's other face:
The dazzling mountains beyond some majestic pines,
The clouds of birds, the Arctic hare, the eagle's resting place,
And dancing Northern Lights—one and all of God's designs.

Long miles, long gruelling miles, then more long miles to forge:
All day up the Alaska Range, another day down
And woe to the team that takes the downhill Dalselle Gorge
In semi-light—for huge rocks will not let you go aroun';

Then across frozen lakes and rivers and the Burn,
Ninety miles of burnt trees stretching forever;
On to ghostly Iditarod but not to sojourn
For there's more endless tundra and Yukon River;

Nearly two hundred miles within this iceberg valley
And on to the Bering Sea—seemed it would never come;
Across the Norton Sound where a storm suddenly
Could trap you out in the open—it's happened to some.

In the silence there was only the muffled swish
Of the runners and the panting of the team—
Puffing out vapour trails, and now his only wish
Was to reach Nome safely—now this became his dream;

Safely to Nome with Silver the ever crafty leader
And Josey and Fleet who faithfully followed in "swing",
Next came the "team" dogs, Skeet, Pistol, Blitz and Hammer,
Followed by Turbo and Rush with power and spring.

All were fast and strong pullers and he loved them all;
As the miles slipped slowly by—he recalled the years
Of training and how they'd saved him from many a fall;
Now watching their valiant efforts brought forth cold tears.

Running mightily through sunshine, sleet and storm,
It's a lot to ask for—twenty hard hours a day.
So they're reluctant to awake in the black morn,
And injuries and cramps will stop some along the way.

One hour of sleep in three days—a sick dog in the sled.
Nome! like a mirage, the flags, banners and crowds appeared.
Soon no more running in pain, no more legs of lead;
Now the hellish trail and its surprises no longer feared;

Now unbelievable—the unending trip was over.
The crowds grew louder and Nome larger, leaving behind:
The fatigue, and delirium. But to recall forever:
The fickle Weather Monster; the Eskimos so kind;

The sight of the heavens on fire—the Northern Lights;
Their crash at Dalsalle Gorge—like a half mile free fall;
Heading out at fifty below into black stormy nights;
And pummelled by coastal winds like a solid wall.

Under the ceremonial arch he threw his snow hook,
Ignoring cheers of loved ones he hugged his team there;
They knew when they had won or lost—it was in their look;
They knew dog and master could trust each other anywhere.

When camped at starry night around the languid fire,
The haunting warble of the dogs seems to say:
They recall the communion and have but one desire
To return to suffer the trail another day.

No Rockin' Chariot for Me

Old rockin' chair's not goin' to git me
No sirree!
No creepin' cane for me
I'm goin' a long way
Somewhere
Somehow
Here on Earth.
Not goin' to ride that rockin' chariot,
You're just a one way ticket
To the bone yard:
Just a dead-end my friend.

Lord don't hold me down;
Goin' to buck up ma heels.
They can't take the life out of me
For I plan to keep on a dancin' and a clownin'.
Ma bones may creek;
Ma feet may cry defeat;
Ma joints may be weak;
Ma brain not fleet;
But ma heart will be light,
And each sunrise and sunset pure delight.

There's goin' to be a long wait for me—
Like Old Man River
I'll keep on a rollin' along—
With a smile and a song.
And if the Pearly Gates gits me
I'll only enter a kickin' and a screamin'.
For I wish to make it clear as clear can be:
With the Jehovah Witnesses
There's one thing we do agree,
"We like it here."

The Why and the Wherefore

It's a mind boggling world we live in
So many whys and wherefores—and where to begin?
The study of the metaphysical and metapsychological
Indicates the world and its people are oft illogical.

Some questions are sure perplexing
To make the brain to go on vexing.
But the more lofty we leave to the Einsteins no less,
Like who created God and why evil exists without redress,
While the trickier issues we humbly address:

Why is it so difficult to locate a mate—
To a pair of socks? And why is this so frequent?
Where will you find it?
You'll find it in the world of the misfit.

Why not turn the mountainous national debt into a pimple
By printing more money and pay it off—wouldn't that be simple?

Why do too many look after their TV and cars better than their bodies
Of sugar and lard?—while joggers glide by with graceful ease.
Why is the favourite household instrument the TV hand control?
We can only surmise for those couch potatoes life must be droll.

Why do drivers become like Jekyll and Hyde behind the wheel?
As either sex turns into a maniac often unreal.

Would a bumble bee fly if it knew it was not designed to fly?
Since it flies anyway, is there a chance for you and I?

Why do male sea lions leave their mates several months a year?
For adventure of course.
Wouldn't this life style be ideal also for humans to avoid divorce?

Since three things are certain in life: taxes, death and junk mail,
Why has the government not thought to tax junk mail without fail?

Since oil and vinegar are compatible,
Then would not wed of an engineer and a nurse still be possible?

Why do they not issue Oscars to the professional wrestlers?
Do they not suffer, boast and cry better than Hollywood actors?

Why does a barber not understand request for a trim?
He wants me back soon, but still he clips, till I'm slim.

Why are there few workers of miracle?
Except perhaps the lawyers who make something out of naught of all they tackle.

Why in 2650 BC did the Chinese come up with 47,035 complex writing characters
of honourable mention when simplicity is the best solution.
There's only one explanation: Complexity was their intention.
Forty-six centuries later they've still not learned: simplicity is the mother of invention.

It's all too stupefying and perplexing—the why and the wherefore;
A conundrum for sure—for the answers guess I'll go to the TV some more.

A Walk with Winter

The outdoors beckons eagerly,
A shining morn with blanket white.
Each slow step brings new life
From the soft caressing wind
And brisk air.
Through the woods I stride—
In wonderment.
The air filled with aroma of pine
And the beauteous chorus
Of joyous fowl.
I wish the woods will never end.
But now into the valley,
Where the sun dances
In the gurgling river.
All is warm and dazzling bright.
Here and there would-be fishermen
Are seen trying their silent luck.
While down the glittering hills,
Toboggans spin and glide—
In merry confusion.
For the dizzy riders there is no time to bide.
The air rings with glee—
And sounds of spirits free.
Sights of fathers and sons
Rolling in the snow—
Here, there, everywhere.

With jealous heart I recall,
That once was me and mine.
Not long ago we laughed,
We also played,
In the sun.
Too soon carefree boys grow to solemn men,
Leaving only a distant memory . . .
With this aching thought,
My steps become heavy—
Homeward bound,
While the winter day suddenly becomes chilled
And no longer filled with glee.

Take Me Back to Wild Calgary

Inspired by many wild parties

First pardner amble into a romping Stampede party;
The room is gyrating as booze flows amid frivolity;
Even staid Easterners are welcome here to share the cheer,
As arms they link with Westerners and friends held dear.

Now we're up and early in spite of fuzzy head
And into crisp air—it's quite a life after all is said.
Ah! the drifting aroma of bacon and coffee
And pancakes out back of covered wagons—what ecstasy.

The Stampede parade is Calgary's welcoming mat;
A million tourists topped by white or black ten gallon hat;
Watch red coated Mounties, clowns, Indians in beaded costume,
And majestic horses dressed in golden harness and plume.

Hear the thousand hoof beats from ponies frisky and stallions stocky,
Ridden by cowgirls so pretty and cowpunchers so cocky;
Bronc riders from Aussiland and vaqueros from Mexico you'll find.
Now thrill to the shrill bands to stir and clear the mind.

The fifty-two acre fairgrounds is beckoning in the searing sun;
From afar the dust and din bespeak of something for everyone;
Thousands of livestock are primed for a four-legged fashion show;
And in the gambling tent your money will go fast so bet low.

Or if your pleasure is to play on rides with Acceleration
Then rise up to see the view on high, if you can pay attention.
See below the Elbow River, huge air balloons, Indian tepees,
Black bears, smiling faces, and lumberjacks rolling on pine with ease,

And the roaring Stadium where Fear and Death is daily defied,
Where thousands admire, stare and share in their mind each daring ride;
Where man's heart and skill are thrust against huge beasts not to be denied,
Where bucking horses and bulls, twist, turn, and pirouette with pride;

Aptly named animals Cyclone, Thunder, Satan or Calamity
Defy the daring riders, for the eight seconds of eternity;
With wild abandon they do it all, bare back, saddle bronco ridin',
Steer wrestlin', chuck wagon and barrel racin' and calf ropin'.

To be thrown skyward a hundred times is not too much;
Promise of fifty-thousand bucks is worth flirting with a crutch.
Then there's the real hero, the clown oft' saving a fallen rider;
By flirting with Danger the frantic bronc or bull they do deter.

Much too soon it's sunset. Suddenly! They're off at the bell—
Thirty-two steeds thundering around the Half Mile of Hell;
The infield is a maelstrom of activity and dust,
While the Stadium springs alive and roars as if to bust.

Each team with four speedy steeds, a wagon, and four riders charging,
Having thrown their stoves and tent poles into the wagons flying—
Are skidding around the barrels—then churning up the track.
But in the prelims two horses were maimed never to come back,

One unlucky wagon lost a wheel but managed to finish still,
And two unrelenting wagons collided causing a spill.
When the final race is run—the hearts of man and beast all sadden,
For wild west stampede fever is over but never forgotten:

Still we hear the clinking glasses and laughing friends in Western dress,
Riders yelping, crowd whooping, rattle of wagons and harness,
And hoof beats pounding above the roaring and revelry.
We taste, we live it up, where life is never dreary.
Oh! take me back, take me back again, to wild Calgary.

Cowboy's Last Ride to Forever

Death wanted him,
His time was up;
With no time for hymn.
Caught in the stirrup
On Death's stallion,
Charging to Forever
For an eon,
Maybe to Despair,
Maybe to Nowhere,
Or God's Stable up there.
Some things are fer sure:
This ride's premature,
Gotta be insecure,
And gonna be a long one . . .
Son-of-a-gun.

Where Eagles Soar

When a fledgling they learned:
To glide . . . from craggy heights
To feel the magic of their wings,
To sense the freshness of flight,
Then to conquer the invisible currents,
Then soar to the stars.
The mountains, oceans, forests and fields
became their playground.
Flying to and fro, high and low—
Feeling high, feeling free—
Knowing the heavens were theirs.

At dawn soaring over misty silent forest—
Giant trees mere blades of grass far below.
At dazzling mid-day drifting over bejeweled
ocean—a muffled snore below.
At sunset watching their mountain home
turning to gold
At night the silence of nothingness—
soothed by white stars more plentiful
than rain drops,
And a brilliant moon shimmering on the water
below—
Transforming to silver—rivers, lakes, and
ocean.
Day and night lording over the world:
Ethereal in flight, reveling in flight, effortless
in flight.
With introspective eye taking in all for
miles around.
Soaring from snow peak—down to ocean roar.
Suddenly! the ultimate dive bomber,
Dropping like a cannonball—
Then flowing swift as the wind in tall grass . . .
to unsuspecting prey.
All the while feeling in their breasts,
But not knowing—this is heaven.

If there is an after-life,
If I have to come back,
I pray Lord—make me an eagle.

The Heavenly Hymn

Did you see them swaying,
Swaying, gently, in the wind?
The stately poplars.
Listen—
Did you hear them singing?
The rush and rustle of a billion leaves
In constant swish and sway
For fifty years or more.
Each leaf alive, dancing, sparkling in the sun,
Playing with the breeze from dawn to dusk,
Then shining under silver moon,
Murmuring lazy in the dark.
They speak in undulating voice—
Oft'times low as if resting;
Then sing in uplifting glorious chorus.
I love to crane upwards—
Engulfed in their whispering:
As relaxing as the lapping and washing
Of endless waves on ocean shore.
Listen—
You'll hear them whisper to your soul.

Reluctantly I bid, "Adieu oh mighty trees!"
They seem to say,
"Pray you'll come another day
To hear our heavenly hymn."

The Perfectionist

I have a friend who's perfect in every way:
Won't drink, smoke, or overindulge
in any way;
Goes to bed at 11;01pm and rises at 7:02 am;
No coffee for him, no drugs of any kind for him;
Clothes wrinkle free, immaculate in every way—
As he swings into his regimented day;
A four P person: punctual, pecuniary, particular
and always perfect
In action, speech and thought;
And never a mistake, and never a risk.
In short—the most boring, uninteresting,
Only a mother could love, person I know.
Problem is—too perfect.
Hard to love one so pure;
Hard to embrace someone so sure.
He can have his four P's—
I say it's pathetic and pitiable.
Some say (not me): never trust:
A bird watcher,
A boy scout leader,
A used car salesman,
Someone about to do you a favor,
Or a man who want drink a drop.
I say never trust a perfectionist or one who
will not take a risk;
But give me someone who's sometimes risky,
Who admits to faults and failure;
But with the inner confidence to learn, forget,
and forge on.
Someone imperfect; but happy, free and easy,
not pesky or picky.
Someone just like you and me.

The Forever Dive

They awaited the call, young faces and old eyes,
To soar on high in their killing machines
In the azure void, where sometimes an angel flies.

Dressed to jump and scramble at the fateful call
In Mae Wests, loose boots, helmet and goggles at hand,
And some with lucky charms for Death to forestall.

Conversation of sticky Op's, ditchings, and prangs,
And happy words of popsies at the local pub,
But forced laughter in this hut where fear lurks and hangs.

The Op's call brings silence and starts the hearts to race.
Yes, it's Jerry approaching the milky coast . . .
Out over the grey green channel at rapid pace.

The aerodrome springs to life in the misty dawn;
Black figures race to grey planes already revving;
While a flare path glimmers with lights in echelon.

The angel wings of darkness still flutter,
Revealing a faint hint of crimson glory,
As Spits shoot skyward as arrows from a quiver.

Now at thirty-thousand into God's ball of fire
The young pilots pray behind their snarling Rolls engines:
One thousand horses, and eight oiled guns that never tire.

Still while searching for Jerry some return
In their thoughts to the pub filled with warm smoke,
Cheerful noise, pots of beer, and to lovers that yearn.

One dreams of Yvonne—will he feel her kiss again?
One longs for Sharmane—to feel her embrace once more,
But others think only of doom, fear and pain.

But all too soon, "Bandits! bandits three o'clock
Just below chaps, tally ho, attack at will."
For a few it would be there last deadly stalk.

For Charlie assigned to the task of "weaver":
Back and forth at the rear better to spot Jerry,
These were searing words in this his first Op ever.

Still there was time for a short prayer," God help me"
As he used to do just before a county race
When adrenalin and heart beat soared in necessity.

But in this stark moment adrenalin burst
Its bounds like water bursting a dam and cold fear
Struck! like an icicle into a brain accursed.

Suddenly! He glimpsed a masked face of the enemy
Behind the black cross on the ME 109;
Like a ghost it was gone, dropping and springing free;

His Spitfire now diving, soaring, and darting
In pursuit, the turns exerting tons of stress
On body and machine; now with strength departing,

As he dove for the clouds in a plunge for life
With the German juggernaut behind him,
His mind flashed back to a carefree time of no strife,

When so proudly watched his mother and father
As he dove from the championship high tower—
Clean as a bullet into the shining water.

Miles below from white cliffs the noisy killing machines
Like attacking hornets are seen with transfixed awe.
Suddenly they're gone and a strange silence contravenes.

Now weird white skeins of contrails fill the sky:
The entrails of combustion that tells a tale
Of the deadly feats of young men not eager to die.

And one lone parachute drifts aimlessly above—
From out of a cloud where one had hoped for refuge,
But where an angel now wraps the lost one in wings of love.

A Smile Pass It On

It costs you nought, achieves much, and cannot be bought;
At home, at work, with friends, it is widely sought.
It cures a tired soul, mends a discouraged mind;
You are rich when in each hour a smile you find.

When its magic beams—the world is brighter by far;
With it there is no beguile or need to spar;
It warms the heart, and melts away fear and distrust;
You must agree to show true love it is a must.

A life of smiles is full and you're sure to win
When your face tells a tale of a sweet soul within.
But a bitter life full of snarls and scowls,
Gives a countenance of wrinkles and clenched jowls.

When a friend has lost their luck or lost a dear one,
Your downcast look will send them on the run.
But your smile can send them to a calm sun-kissed beach
And then carefree tranquil days seem within reach.

Now when you meet a stranger who is down and out,
Don't ignore or give him another nasty clout.
A smile may lift him to struggle on awhile;
With renewed hope he goes the extra mile.

One warm smile can grow and multiply if passed on,
From friend to friend, friend to stranger, hither and yon;
Don't miss an opportunity from dawn to dawn.
A happier world there will be—pass it on!

The Mighty Sauble Elm

Located near Wyreton and Sauble Beach in Ontario, Canada
Photo shows a smaller (15 foot circumference white oak) tree
in Oakville Ontario.

The three-hundred year old Sauble Elm shrieked in pain;
Each rush of the saw severing its monstrous trunk,.
bringing a scream of waning life
and a step closer to eternity.
Who would have dreamt it would grow so big from a small twig?
This Goliath a full twenty feet in circumference—
with its top in the heady clouds—
on the banks of the Sauble River near the mighty Lake Huron,
but killed in the year nineteen-sixty-eight in one tortuous hour.
As David slew Goliath, a microcosmic germ had
fatally sickened this forest giant cutting of its food supply;
otherwise it would be standing still.
For some seconds it tottered—
unwilling to fall and die—
gravity prevailed and with a terrible tearing—,
through smaller brothers—that seemed to last forever . . .
as if in slow motion it angled earthward . . .
landing with a crash—
of resounding thunder heard for miles around—
causing the earth to quake
as it bounced on the forest floor.
Some of the forest laughed and some cried to see this friendly giant down
and its limbs twisted so.

Then the wind took up a horrible wailing through the trees,
wracked in anxiety and sorrow,
along with the weeping of the river,
and crying of winged friends.
For three centuries of history, it had reigned like an immortal monarch
through peace, wars and bloodshed;
Used as a landmark guiding Indians to their villages;
And used as a beacon guiding birds to their nests.
From on high it saw the fires of Indian encampments
like fire flies in the night;
Sighted the occasional Jesuit missionary
and courier de bois from New France;
Then saw below the bustle of lumbermen and teams of horses tiny as ants
destroying the peace with thumping of razor sharp axes,
shrieking of saws,
crashing timber and warning cries;
Watched as many a small brother fell under the cruel axe
after shielding them from birth;
Then heard the screaming saws in the distant sawmills
and the steamboats plugging and plying slowly in the swollen river;
And occasionally witnessed gigantic fires in the distance.
But no more it's life blood flowing;
No more the music of a million leaves murmuring;
No more the home, refuge, and lookout for a thousand birds;
No more to survey the wide river
or the forest in its several robes
through icy blasts and yellow sunshine;

No more to reign magnificent in its own colourful cloak;
No more to be held in awe.
Farewell King of the forest, lakes, rivers, hills, and flowers.
Reign no more!
Your smaller younger brothers now bid farewell
  to a courageous friend and guardian:
  their past comfort through days of sun, shower and wicked wind.
Nothing lasts forever, not even the Sauble Elm;
It was a long solitary, silent, patient life;
Farewell oh gentle goliath!
It was time—as for all things—
To die.

Apache Boy versus the Desert

Ocheewan had moved rapidly on moccasined feet
While avoiding the rocks and pines of the mountain canyon;
The white moon had shown the way out to the desert floor
As the stars danced in the stillness and held sovereignty
Over the sombre canyon walls.
In the cocoon of night he felt secure,
But his senses were ever alert for the enemy.
He was an Apache Indian—but fifteen—
In the year eighteen-sixty-three
With a man's task: to run seventy miles to his village;
To save his father, brother Taza and two other warriors
Pinned down at the waterhole.

As night threw its cloak over the stars and retreated,
The flickering dawn approached cautiously.
When he emerged into the desert it seemed:
Haunted by phantoms,
Low lying dark shrubs,
Shadowy cacti,
And overlooked by the brooding mountains.
In the semi-darkness his pace quickened;
As the dark shrubs turned to green
His mind raced back to the past two nights;
Through his fatigue he could not erase:
Leaving the village with the raiding party;
His mother crying and fearing their deadly mission;
After one-hundred miles or more stealing the Mexican ponies;
Stopping at the waterhole in the quiet canyon;
The ambush and release of all the horses by the Mexicans;
With no escape possible.

When the dark night brought peaceful respite,
A light breeze, the scent of pines and cedars,
The still white stars, and the howl of coyotes,
His father had asked him to steal away for help,
Or was it to save his son whom he loved more dearly than life.
Sadly Ocheewan left.
Treading lightly, feeling every twig through his moccasins
For the slightest sound travelled easily in the still air;
He crept, disturbing only an owl—
That took off lazily through the stately pines.

Now an ocean of prairie stretched before him
Broken by countless canyons and knolls,
But in the distance appearing as a flat expanse.
He knew the desert and its wrathfulness;
In a few hours it would be a hell hole of heat;
But now the new-borne sun emblazed the sky and sands
With brilliant reds and golds.

This Indian boy did not fear the long run
For it was the Apache way to fight on foot
And race a hundred miles or more in the desert;
But the previous day he had no sleep and only a handful of corn.
Now he ran through fear, as if chased by the Devil himself
Or as an animal flees to save its life.
He floated as graceful as a deer for he loved to run.
After countless races on the plains
He knew what he could do:
Much more than the white man.

Sunrise was two hours gone and the desert sky steel blue and clear,
The sky was everywhere; it overpowered and encompassed all In its enormity,
While below the heat devil was stirring up its ferocious fire.
As Ocheewan had feared the shimmering sun reflected off:
The sparse grass,
The dark junipers,
The occasional canyon,
The interminable desert floor,
And turned the pinks and reds to copper and brass.
From innocent blue the sky was turned into a fearsome inferno
While the horizon was obscured by dancing heat
waves.
He welcomed the cooling effect of his sweat,
But feared his water bag would soon be empty.
Now he would have welcomed the rain and wind that roared
The night of their fateful raid; or welcomed even a small dust demon.

As time passed he was alone except for the energetic lizards
That darted across his path;
Once a proud chaparral cock trotted by;
Then in the distance that stretched forever
The ever patient vultures hung lazily in the sky
Awaiting the inevitable demise of any desert creature
Who dared to exist in this furnace.
Ocheewan was now running in a daze,
Limbs moving automatically,
Alone except for his adversary
The blazing sun on high.
Three hours ago he had thrown down his empty water bag;
The demon dehydration was moving in;
It seemed he could hear only the hum of the heat waves
Dancing to a tortuous tune.
But it was the Apache way to endure
And to be exceedingly brave.
In the oppressive heat his mind drifted
To his tribes treatment of white settlers
Sometimes tied to wagon wheels with a fire beneath their head.
And now an additional burden leapt onto his back:
Fatigue!

The desert floor passed slowly mile by mile;
Twice he had fallen on the rough terrain;
An eternity passed and passed again;
Now with parched mouth,
Limbs burning with lactate,
Feet bruised and bloody,
His thoughts turned to his mother.
Now she would be searching the heat waves to the west
Desperately, hoping for father and son to appear on the horizon;
By now her whole body would be a torrent of fear
Filled with black thoughts of death.
He dreaded to pass his dark message.

Long hours past high noon an enquiring quail called to bid
Hello! and quickly sped away;
Now he knew he was near.
And then it was there—the deep Blue River he knew so well
Where the tall grass waved welcome in long ripples;
He saw the bright sun bless the white tepees;
The happy smoke rising in thin streams in the still air;
Then heard laughing children and barking dogs.
His man's task was nearly done;
He knew he was home, but his trial not over.
Could they return in time? Could he find his way back?

Nowhere to Run, Nowhere to Hide

We set for England—a mighty fleet,
All in zig zag course . . .
A longer but safer way across.
Forty large and small vessels, eight abreast:
Potbellied tankers, converted liners, ships bristling with troops,
Liners that sailed thousands of miles in happy sunny times.
There would be some great days with the bad:
Gray silhouettes on glittering sea
Leaving behind white foam trails;
And even calm nights with myriad shimmering stars—
More plentiful than grains of sand on a beach—
Keeping vigil over the silent flock.
On calm days straining, looking for a periscope
The Cyclops of the enemy;
Searching for a needle in a haystack.

Thirty-nine crossings to and from England for me,
Maybe my time is up this trip,
Maybe I would feel the icy ocean again.
Strange how a prairie boy landed in the Navy,
Joined for a job,
But my stomach never got use to the rocking and rolling,
Still I did my job.
I remember waves seventy-five feet high in Artic gales,
The creaks and vibrations—the rocking and rolling.
Sometimes three weeks to cross this heaving—grey green monster:
A monster that could turn abruptly into a merry maiden.
Sometimes not moving for days waiting for the storm to die . . .
Sitting ducks but difficult to see in these mountain waves.
Then too often in winter our vessel icing up:
Tons of it threatening to pull us under or tip us over,
As we fought frantically for our lives with pick and axe.
Each day filled with monotony, and fear of dying so young,
For death might be lurking behind any wave
And in front of every torpedo.
When close to death every day
You get close to God and your mates.
Yes, most of us did a lot of praying,
But it was a realistic fear:
Fear of the power of Mother Nature, and of the U-boats;
Yes, we had respect for the power of these vultures of the sea;
We even dreaded a calm clear day feeling like vulture meat for the picking;

Dreaded a calm day—foreboding a giant storm
And longed for the safety of a moonless night.
We prayed that any white fish in our direction was not acoustic,
To home into the "thrump—thrump—thrump" of our churning screw.
But on my twelfth crossing it happened one black night:
Our ship carrying bunker oil was struck becoming a flaming beacon;
Our ship broken at the spine and with boilers burst;
I still remember the stench of human flesh;
We struggled in the thick oil and frigid water for four hours under a veiled smoke screen,
Before the destroyers could finish their frantic
chasing,
scrambling,
spurting charges side to side
to a hidden quarry,
and get to me and the other lucky survivors.
Yes we prayed a lot that time.
But still we're here—some of us.
Some poor souls joined the ghosts of the past
In an icy grave as millions before.

There was some comfort in the other neighboring vessels,
And the few swift destroyers—our diligent watch dogs on the outer rim,
To engage slippery U-boats in a deadly chess game.
But small consolation when outnumbered by a U boat wolf pack of fifteen or more.
They could get under and inside our outer boundary.
And there was nowhere to run and nowhere to hide.

We dreamed—of a night of beer, laughter and women
At the Pig and Whistle in Portsmouth—a fortnight away—
Our Port of Dreams.
We could feel the warmth of many bodies:
We could hear the loud chatter and laughter;
And we longed for the smell of booze and smoke.
Such thoughts and of our loved ones kept us going.

Adventure is fine—say what you will,
But living beats adventure every time—this I know.
Only a fool would think otherwise.
Yes! we did a lot praying, and I'm here to tell the tail—
Thank God!

High Rollers

The sunny silence-
Of lazy summer-
Is shattered!
By the rumbling of hard plastic wheels
On hot concrete.
I peer from my open window
To the once serene street below,
To see two weird tricycles
Flying by- rolling from on high
Down the hill so steep.
The race is on!
A flash of yellow wheels,
A blurr of purple wheels,
In close proximity
And two gleeful boys
Carefree- in gaiety;
Heads on high;
Their long screams muffled by the roar;
Playing with their pal Gravity,
Roll, roll, rumble, roar,
Now do it some more;
Spin yellow wheels, spin purple
Shining in the gleaming sun.

Can there be more delight
When there is naught fright?
As I watch-
With envy,
Sweet memories of youth returns;
Oh! to relive it just for one hour.
I turn my gaze,
In melancholy
From two lads in gaiety,
Playing with Gravity,
To the thought:
How blissful are innocent souls
Without worldy cares!

Jet Streams and Dreams

Thin white contrails in the dazzling azure sky
crisscrossing,
making a checkerboard in the air.
Tiny black dots at 500 miles per hour
carrying hundreds of dreams:
fresh dreams to dead dreams.
Some speeding to their dream,
Some retreating hangdog from a cold hand
of crashed hopes,
Some with dreams as lively as an Olympic flame,
Some with selfish dreams or with dreams to share,
Some eager to grasp them with steel talons,
But many caring not or knowing not what to grasp for:
these the fun lovers,
the drifters, the bored,
the insecure, the humdrum,
the hopeless, the listless,
the deplorables.
And most rushing onwards to reach their end before:
the fame, the riches, or the love,
in their dream.
Many have cast off their heady hopes—
a coat too leaden for life's stream,
For a dream untended can escape . . .
Like a balloon released to the heavens . . . forever.

Happiness Is a Butterfly

Pine not for things you have not.
You gotta look after what you've got
And like what you can get,
Even though it's not a lot.

A grasp too greedy oft turns to grapes of wrath
And crushed dreams.
So you see—Bernard was not too foxy.
And don't dwell on "if only,"
If only, is just soap bubbles bursting in air.

A nun asked my friend Louise shortly after major
surgery:
"What is curing you?"
"Laughter!" she replied. That is happiness.
A pessimist awakened by the morning rays
and chattering birds says:
"Blasted birds!"
But a contented man says: "Another blessed Godly
day, sing on my little friends."

What is the secret of contentment?
Peace within,
Laughter,
Count your blessings,
Loved ones,
Love of nature,
Health not wealth,
Optimism,
Love, love, love.
I tell you truly,
Happiness is a butterfly—
Hard to catch if pursued
Incessantly.
But if contented then happiness
Will alight—
Upon your shoulder.

Sharing the Forest Cathedral

Based on an experience in Erindale University woods,
December 1989

In the white stillness,
The frozen earth and new born snow,
Crunch, and crunch again,
Under my flying feet;
The pine trees flit by—
With fragrance divine;
My breath in ghostly wisps,
Drifts upwards—
Lost in the crystal branches of this
forest cathedral.

Swiftly I pick my way,
Along the path so winding—
A gentle rise, a gentle fall
And around each bend another beauteous
wonder;
Now into an open meadow—a soft white
blanket.
And then there they are!
Eight creatures of God—innocent deer,
Peering in wonderment at me,
While at peace with the world and mankind.

Unslowing my pace remains,
I'm unwilling to stand and stare.
Some common interests in God's handiwork we
share,
And in hearts that beat,
Arising from a common pursuit—
To float with grace and light feet;
Theirs is my goal to emulate.
So follow the river far below
Onwards at a breathless rate.

On my weary return the shadows darken
And the quiet meadow is now bathed in pink,
But they are gone—except one;
This gentle soul remains and approaches near;
As I drift by there is no retreat or fear.
Now my heart is gladdened,
My pace quickens and is more sure
At this act of trust and friendliness kind
By a fellow creature,
As my unflagging feet leave the forest cathedral
far behind.

The Wind Chimes

The phone call came at four in the morning;
This time of day never brings good news,
My heart was racing,
"Our mother has died, come down to the
apartment."
My older brother, a loner, always stoic, was the
same today.
On the way driving in the blackness to the city
at sleep
I clung to the slim hope,
Maybe they're teaching me a lesson:
I had not been much in contact after my
marriage
For reasons beyond my control.
But no it was true as I feared:
No one had noticed her absence for three days
In the summer city heat.
The few hours following were a blur.
Then there were the relatives and friends
packing the belongings,
A hard task in view of the memories
in each and every thing;
Packing was too much for me as I wandered
around in a daze.

The wind chimes in the window facing St Clair
Street
were the last to go;
These I particularly related to her
And the many happy times there:
the serene,
calm,
warm,
comfortable,
loving,
laughter times,
Always taken for granted,.
Never thinking these times would never last.
With tears I said, "Let's leave them."
But they tore them down.
Now the carefree
tinkling,
tinkling—
The winds of joy in those chimes
Are over forty years gone,
But the memories and the music still blow
wistfully
on and
on . . ..

Candy Floss Trees

It's spring making my spirits to soar—
As I stand entranced in warm golden rays
At a joyful sight just outside my door,
For down the hill lining my street is a blaze
Of pink and red blossoms everywhere.
For some days it's been a carnival
Of excitement; each day I stand and stare
At ten parent apple trees standing tall,
And eight daughters all bursting in bloom;
The mature trees in soft pinks are dressed,
Like candy floss at the circus they loom,
While youngsters in brilliant red are blest.

Today millions of pink petals like confetti
Cover the grey pavement all down the hill.
Such beauty is too short lived—what a pity!
It's another example of God's will.
But if this rare pleasure were here always,
Appreciation of it would surely fade.
But happily the young trees will amaze
A few more rosy days, then also jade.
Farewell my faithful friends till your return
Next year to bring again God's painting.
I hope to recall this scene when concern
Of winter's grasp brings on yearning for spring.
Alas the pink petals fall much too soon,
But the pink on black sings a happy tune.

The Flower Lady in the Oasis

The basic idea of this poem came from a similar poem by poet/friend Wayne Cosgrove

I stepped inside to the din of the market;
Here were hundreds clamouring to avoid debt,
In search of bargains in many a ware
And not knowing what surprises were awaiting there:
Pig's tails next to bananas, next to trinkets,
Antiques old and new, and even some pets,
Paraphernalia for the man who has all,
Something for the woman who wants all,
And all manners of goods in many a stall
Including food to provide bodily sugar and lard.
Hence strange aromas did the nose bombard.
In this jungle of goods, a flowering oasis
In a far corner—a vendor of bliss—
The flower lady—sat amongst the floral hue
Of pink, crimson, orange, purple, white and blue;
Graceful age surrounded by youthful blossoms
And a cart overfilled with chrysanthemums.
All these blooms grown with loving care in her marsh
To bless some home and render life less harsh.
Many faces passed by her stall, the busy,
The angry, disgruntled, melancholy,
The fearful, and even a few quite happy,
And some with overburdened step or unsprightly.
She passed on her beauties for scarce pennies,
With loving hands showing lines of hard ease.
Her profits for more seeds would soon be spent,
But pleased was she to pass on some contentment
And to share her fresh wares with the well and sick.
Those who stopped by—as if by magic
Left with renewed steps, and shining faces—
As the flower lady smiled from her oasis.

Childhood Memories of the West

Pigs as big as horses,
Horses as huge as elephants,
A bull as big as a hippo,
A rooster as ferocious as a lion;
All these caused me fear when I came near,
As I recollect on my days as a tot
Down on the farm near Saskatoon Saskatchewan.

Later as a braver tot chasing my adversary the rooster,
Getting into the tar barrel with brother Maurice,
Gleefully catching gophers at one cent per tail,
Wearily stacking wheat at one cent per stook,
Turning upside down the butter churn and spilling all,
I found adventure and life was never drear
Down on the farm near Saskatoon Saskatchewan.

The prairies like a tamed sleeping giant
With golden silken hair that flows forever in the summer sun,
Underneath a sky unending,
And land so flat the fireworks at the fair a hundred miles away
could be seen,
With only a few forlorn farms or barns dotting the horizon.
It's all with me still—when life was serene and dear
Down on the farm near Saskatoon Saskatchewan.

The monster threshing machines were seen and heard miles away,
Spewing and chugging from dawn till early night.
Ah! those threshing meals—Grandma would cook all day—
The table creaking with mountains of meats, pies and other treats;
After watching all that work even Maurice and I could demolish a pie.
Grandma always sensed when company was coming,
Then she would cook some more.
Then at night Grandad would recite poems like Sam McGee . . .
It wasn't all work you see—
Down on the farm near Saskatoon Saskatchewan.

The winters sometimes fifty below;
Colder than the feel of flesh stuck on chilled steel;
The horses with bells, plunging through snow drifts up to their knees,
Pulling the covered caboose with glowing iron stove,
Rugs, hot rocks, Mama, Daddy and brothers all snug inside;
These I warmly recall of childhood
Down on the farm near Saskatoon Saskatchewan.

Soon I knew the horses were not to be feared but loved;
Grandad boasted of the finest work horses in the world;
But Goldy, Sandy, Fany, Roxy and many others
Were more, much more than beasts of burden;
When the tractors replaced them years later it was the end of an era,
And these faithful friends were sadly missed
Down on the farm near Saskatoon Saskatchewan.

The pain we caused our parents dear
When Maurice and I wandered afar to distant lake,
Pushing a raft like Huckleberry Finn,
But since prairie born we could not swim,
Then straggling home at dark with withered flowers to make amends,
On one of those happy-sad days
In Vonda the tiny town near Saskatoon Saskatchewan.

Those prairie days were too precious to last;
I learned at eight nothing lasts forever.
When we left behind Grandma, Grandad and loving pet Brownie
All down-cast at the Railway Station platform,
Not an eye was dry and I saw for the first time dogs can cry
And have a broken heart too—all this I knew
On moving East, leaving all we loved—behind—in Saskatchewan.

Faces

Every human being carries his life in his face;
The face tells all, so they claim.
The good the evil deposited over the years
Are truly revealed in facial features and ones you deserve.

Many faces once seen are hard to recall
And some a pleasure to forget,
While others remind of a garden where roses and lilies grow;
These we long to know.
And eyes oft'times show less expression than glass
While some eyes speak of a gentle heart and soul within.
The eyes and face liken to a contents page of a book,
Perhaps a whole volume of chicanery or roguery
Or of wrath, hatred, envy, pride, jealousy, love, fear, anger,
Pain, dismay, goodness, pleasure, affection, peace, and wonder.

On the downtown train are many smitten with the Orpheus God
But if one looks with discerning eye at those awake their story within
is sometimes plain.
Here's an individual with Incredulity written all over it
like one who has just received a bill from their custody lawyer.
Here's one with Dejection on the front cover looking like having just lost
their pet poodle.
Here's Sorrow, possibly not looking forward to having the mother-in-law
over for the weekend.
Here's Oblivion, behind jet black glasses, hoping to block out the world.
Here's Sadness, appearing as if welfare cheques had just been cancelled.
Here's Pain and Suffering, possibly a tale of haemorrhoids to the bitter end.
Here's Happiness, with a smiling face guaranteed if it's a young man speaking
to a pretty maid.

Here's The Road Too Long, a face that: needs detreading, worn out several bodies,
been around the world and rolled over by the world.
Here's Miserable, a tale of a wretched countenance, indicating life can be an unbearable dance.
There's a face that's launched a thousand barges,
And here's a face that's lunched a thousand binges.
Here's Trickery, behind those shifty orbs and insincere lips are
a thousand evil deeds while weaving a crooked path of lies and deceit.
Here's Confidence, born from shifting and lifting tons of cold steel,
or highly skilled at something real.
Here's Goodness, the purity that cannot be denied by the eyes,
having scattered a thousand pearls of kindness along the way.
Here's Optimism, with beaming face shedding brightness all around,
making the world a better place.
Here's Pessimism, lurking in a shadow of gloom, making the world seem doom.
Here's Godliness, such a serene face has surely seen God.
Here's Worry, in deep anxiety about what never happens, always meeting
trouble halfway, and shunning gaiety.
Here's Melancholy, the lazy demon which wishes happiness and optimism begone.
Here's Contentment, from the attire it appears not possessing much, but content with such.

Some faces are like books—easy to discern by their cover, but some faces like Beauty and Evil
may wear a mask,
So beware my friends, in case that face is actually fiction.

The Awakening

Suddenly it was here again,
Spring! the birds were home and rejoicing;
Spring! freshness was everywhere;
Spring! energy was charging the air;
Spring! I wanted to embrace it,
to swallow it, to wallow in it,
to roll in it as a pig rolls in mud;
Spring! I wanted it to stay forever,
as one hopes to keep ones offspring young;
Spring! it was a time to pause,
in the sun, to reflect,
on the awe and wonder of it all.
Spring! I was old, but young again.

Cherry Blossoms and Almond Eyes

A golden day experience in High Park, Toronto,

It was spring again
In the warm sun.
I happened by a mountain of blossoms
Just below the top of a green hill.
This glorious sight like a shimmering cloud
Beckoned me on—
Looking down—
Unbelievably a visual treasure:
A galaxy of white and pink petals,
Seeming more frequent than stars,
From dozens of forty year old
Japanese cherry trees
All in bloom.
The brilliance near blinded the eyes.
Strange how such knarled trunks
Could produce such beauty.
An unforgettable sight to behold:
A rising winding path
Lined with a multitude of sentinel trees
Robed in millions of velvety flowers in delicate colours;
At bottom of the hill—a tranquil pond
With gentle swans;
And by the edge weeping willows—
Their strands of golden beads hanging in the sun;
All this against the bright blue sky.
Each passer-by standing in awe
Or walking in silent admiration
Of Gods artistry;
Some lay gazing up into the sea of petals
Peering to the heavens
Wondering what is more beautiful
The blossoms or the azure sky?
Besides it was spring again
With the sun blessing the skin.

I thought this nature was beyond compare,
Till I met here the girl with the almond eyes;
The blossoms faded away while she was there.

Her words were gentle without beguile,
The girl I met with the bewitching smile;
Her ways will last forever and a while.

Like a petal her ways were soft as gentle rain,
But I lost the girl with the almond eyes;
When petals fall and die—she'll long remain.

The Bull Rider

A strange breed are they—the daredevil bull rider.
Roped in solid straining every sinew—
Riding a hurricane or whirlwind would be easier.
The gate swings open—each animal an experience new—
Cyclone, Baby Face, Sweety Pie, Calamity, and Big Red
Many they've maimed,
And beware of some not aptly named, and some too aptly named.
Seven seconds—an infinity to the bell;
It could be heaven or it could be hell
While a thousand pounds of muscle pirouettes, twists, and contorts—
They have the knack;
Greatly determined to rid this pest from off their back;
Kicking its back heels eight feet above the ground;
Thousands are cheering but extreme concentration blocks all sound
For both rider and bull. Man against beast it's a fair contest
And beast never suffers; they know their job the best.
But man—cracked ribs, broken teeth, fractured limbs—he's had it all,
Oft'times kicked, trampled, bounced and tossed like a limp rag doll
To the heavens. But just to escape could seem grand
Especially when trapped by the rope and feet dancing in the sand.
Why any man would play this insane game of tricks
Is a mystery—but that's how these bull dogs get their kicks.

The Swan

The Lord had finished His comical frame of mind
Having just created animals of a wierd kind;
Like hippopotomus, giraffe, kangaroo,
Armadillo and camel to mention a few.

Now tired—the Creator sought some peaceful time—
Meanwhile the angels had started a chorus sublime;
But a bird of purity was in his dream,
Of downy white like sunny clouds all agleam.

He could see the neck so elegant and beyond compare;
He could hear the huge wings humming in the air;
Wings to glorify and cover the body perfect;
Angellic wings for flight and powerful to protect.

In the blood of this great bird He could feel love and grace.
The picture was complete and a creation in place,
Not born with fire and sudden lightning in the veins—
As an eagle—but from calm and starry nights where peace reigns.

Of all His species non would surpass this paragon,
To adorn our world and for all to marvel on and on.

The Weeping Angel

The weeping angel on Harris grave at Mount Pleasant gate
Epitimizes it all for the unknown to the great,
And the cherished ones remembered in stone, marble and brass;
For they'll tread and grace our gay green world no more—alas.

Everywhere you will find loved ones laying side by side;
With their mate gone the other can no longer abide
The lonely void with nought to relieve a shattered heart;
Strangely but willingly too soon after they too depart.

In spring when the earth awakens and abounds in newborn love;
In summer when sprightly flowers speak of the Above;
In autumn when flying leaves form a magic carpet;
And when winter spreads its white blanket—we will not forget.

Carefree Country

In the crowded metropolis
There's stress and smog—
and here this:

There are a few devotee,
But you'll find little pity.

Problem is nature is lacking,
Therefore the soul is not singing.

The universe is never there—
At night—too much city glare.

You're lucky to see a lone star,
It's a universe too far.

A golden sunset or sunrise?
No! too much concrete for these eyes.

In the metropolis
It's the country I miss.

Neighbours helpful and kind,
Sharing burdens you'll find.

Do you not agree in the country
You feel carefree—ah c'est la vie.

The Pitiful Composer

The nights are long and lonely
Like the woeful wail of a freight train
Way out on the prairies.
Then only dreams remain;
I'm off in strange silent scenes
And hushed foreign lands
In a deaf world.
With strange bedfellows experiences bizarre I share:
Loved ones of yesteryear appear;
And love pangs and past happy times return as before;
Some unknowns arrive, it's instant attraction,
Stirring up new love, too long buried.
The subterranean mind,
A poor pitiful composer,
Composes and directs:
With disjointed stories,
Weak nonsensical plots,
In jumbled scenes,
While juggling characters old, new and strange.
Then in the all-too- welcome morn
On awakening to reluctant light . . .
I live it all again . . .
Unable to comprehend it all.
But now the woeful wail of the freight train
Is way off in another world.

The White Wonder

The whiteness started as a flake or two
Then billions and billions filling the gray air—
Filling the branches of every tree
Roof tops, roads, fences and lawns
Valleys, groves, hills and fields, woods
Streams, lakes and rivers.
Not like the robust cousins:
the noisy clattering rain
and the shattering hail
on tin roofs.
But softly, gently, quietly, falling
Filling each and every crevice
Painting all in white.
Creeping on muffled feet like a giant white cat
Turning brown and black and green to white
All is whiteness and silence and all is calm.
The quiet deafening.
Now the sun burst forth
Bringing a multitude of jewelled crystals
in the trees—
And everywhere gigantic white mounds
like rich ice cream:
Wondrous but blinding to look upon;
Wondrous to romp in, to fall in, to throw, to play in.
Bringing back youthful, carefree, crispy days
in the snow and ice and the sun.
And I'm young once again.

The Maples of Port Elgin

Many a morn I hear the honking geese
Flying in their V to the shore—ah peace!
They're out over the giant trees of Port Elgin
At sunrise with God's ball of fire rolling in.

Long ago there were five-thousand and one seeds:
A seed of a dream and five-thousand seeds
Of Maple to disperse along each street
And byway where beauty and solitude meet.

'Twas a dream nearly a hundred years away,
But some saw the Maples as giants one day.
It's sad the dreams came too late
For the dreamers—for indeed it was a long wait.

Made from servant earth and rain, wind and sun—
From a tiny seed its life begun;
Surviving the winter's terrible blast
With winds that scream and snows that last and last.

Streets of dreams, streets of dreams, east and west,
North and south, streets of dreams, all were blest,
On each side by long grey boughs with leafy manes
Forming temple-like vaults in shady lanes.

Now! full thirty meters high and ten meters apart
These gentle giants fail not to warm the heart;
Their mossy trunks gnarled and massive of physique
Like ancient bearded faces—they try to speak,

Of generations of lovers that passed;
Of horse and carriage and sleigh of the past;
Of music of the wind and smiles and tears;
And evil storms that tore their limbs for years.

In truth these Maple goliaths have neighbours fine;
Like the swaying Willow and Silent Pine,
The soft rustling Poplar and mighty Oak.
When we think of these—Heaven we invoke.

When I return to home they're there to greet me,
Giving a feeling of warm security
Within each wondrous canopy—then, to my delight
The murmuring of dancing leaves soothes the night.

The trees by day bathed in light of one lone star
And by night by millions smiling from afar—
Set their watch as sentinels in the streets
Until faded darkness and daylight meets.

And now that autumn is creeping near
I know they'll paint a picture to endear,
One of rainbow colors, a kaleidoscope,
To soften even a heart bereft of hope.

What a desolate world there would be
Without the sight and sound of a tree.
It would be happiness without the smiles;
A life without love—through long lonely miles.

Till the Last May You

May you rise up eager in the morning,
And live each precious day like your last;
May you stay forever young;
May you give more than you get;
May they recall you as a giver and not a taker;
May you prize loved ones and your own shining temple
More than shekels and cars;
May your heart be warm and true;
May you never look down on anybody;
May you say no ill of anyone,
Grandmother told me so.
May you live forever grateful;
May your feet be light and have wings;
May you ever run swift and strong as the wind,
And to your opponents say bye bye;
May you win with no bravado
And lose with perfect grace;
May you always know your place
In the palm of His hand;
And may you make the world more beautiful
In passing by.

Till the last dance with your true love;
Till your last drop of fine red wine;
Till that last warm embrace;
Till they ring the bell for your last lap—
The most tiring lap ever;
Till your last fond farewell;
Till you see His glorious face,
The Ultimate Meet Director;
Till you receive your bronze, silver, or golden wings,
May yours be golden;
And may they remember you forever.

LOVE

A Mother's Love

There are some bright stars in Heaven;
Though long gone their light will shine
To Earth for ever and amen;
These are the mothers of yours and mine.

A mother's love is warmer than a fire
After winter's bitter sting;
Soft and tender as an angel's choir
And as comforting as an angel's wing;

The best friend that God ever gave;
Only they could show such patience,
And faith while harsh words they would save,
In hopes of better deeds sometime hence.

Now their warm words are here no more,
But in our memory they speak still,
Like sparkling waves on a sun baked shore
They return, return, to stir our will.

Their lessons and stories are not forgot
In our journey through smiles and tears.
The truth, honour, and virtue they taught
Are with us to conquer our fears.

In yesteryear when we were frail,
They picked us up fall after fall.
And now when we stumble and fail,
Though gone, they are there after all.

Their first great sacrifice of many
Was to enter at our birth,
The black cloak of death valley;
Thereafter all sacrifice was mirth.

We wish to tell her all that she has been;
Her beauty, sacrifice, and tenderness.
Too late now to render conscience serene,
But never too late to recall her fond caress.

Yes, a mother's love is a perfect love
That goes on for evermore.
Someday—we'll meet again up above,
"Else what's a heaven for?"

Mummy

Just a simple message: "Mummy"
On the casket of Diana.
Her life was care, with love to share.
None can replace her grace—her face.
But not really gone, for she lives on
In the misty English air and everywhere.
She touched us all from old to small
In our hearts—forever the "Queen of Hearts."

Down Happy Memory Lane

Old friends from yesteryear—
Think not that I have forgotten.
Our physical paths have diverged,
New different interests,
And now miles apart.
But there is a mental path oft travelled—
Down happy memory lane.
It's hard to forget a loved one;
For I chose not to forget.
Love can linger on and on—
Fortunately,
Forever.

There Is No Tomorrow

There is oft'times no tomorrow while through life we speed.
We think there's no need to express our love in word or deed,
To one of the family, loving friend or relative dear;
They will not be here forever more—that is clear.

Loving thoughts left unspoken oft lead to sorrow;
Time and again, love and affection we fail to show;
It would have taken so little, just some courage,
But too late now, the players have left the stage.

A mother departs Earth and a son writes a tearful letter,
Pouring out in tears how much he respected and loved her;
Now ten thousand voices and letters are of no avail;
Taking for granted our loved ones is where we fail.

My friend plucked up faith and courage one eventful day;
His aging father stood with outstretched hand—farewell to say,
But his son took him in warm embrace—"Father I love you!"
It was years overdue—an act to aspire to.

The Flute that Will Not Die (The Taj Mahal)

A flute blown once within the dome of Queen Mumtaz's tomb,
Continues in countless harmonies and overtones
Amid a hundred arched alcoves in this magnificent room
Of purity, grace and white marble inlayed with precious stones.

The music returns, returns and cast their spell over all,
Over the sarcophagi of Shah Jahan and his queen;
One and all adored her, the beautiful Mumtaz Mahal.
A greater story of romance the world has never seen.

The sonorous echo is the soul to the Taj Mahal,
An undying memory that will not let you be.
Our minds cast back to sixteen-o-seven for a tale to enthral
When prince Khurran at a bazaar met Arjumand and destiny.

To the emperor a request the next day he did make
For permission to marry this girl whose rare beauty so pleased.
Though a marriage of love and passion would be to forsake
Indian customs; but strangely the emperor agreed,

For had he not done the same for Nur Mahal with some sins.
To wed her: her husband, Sher Afghan, he had to kill;
The tiger, the wild elephant, the forty assassins
Were not enough; then a hundred more before his blood did spill.

Five long years, Prince Khurran awaited the stars to agree,
And for five long years the lovely Arjumand he could not see.
Then at long last the marriage procession gracefully swayed
Through throngs of poor from jewelled howdahs on elephants staid.

The prince and princess, emperor, and officials rode on high,
Followed by armies of musicians, acrobats, dancers;
Silver palanquins with veiled ladies tossing coins to the sky;
Painted pygmies carrying yellow parrots and caged panthers;

Sweating coolies with fiery torches lighting the balmy night;
Shining black slaves with elephant ear fans shooing flies;
And everywhere myriad colours the eye to delight;
While drummers played a happy sad cadence with chants and cries.

Arjumand was bestowed as Chosen One of the Palace
And known as Mumtaz Mahal, the beautiful, demure,
Charitable, intelligent, kind, and constant solace
To the prince from his life of affairs of state or torture:

Pastimes like suffocating men in an animal carcass;
Or the prince's favourite diversion, an elephant fight
In the river beds—a battle of pachyderms enormous
With the riders ever praying to survive their plight.

True there were his wives so many, a concubine so busy.
Still the prince's world was Mumtaz—his everlasting love
And constant companion during campaigns peaceful and warly.
His bliss ended when in labour she was lost to Allah above,

Leaving a colossal anguish, after children fourteen
And years nineteen. For three brief years she had been his queen
But now the emperor's throne he had killed for and sought
Was bitter solace to the Shah; in his grief all was for nought.

Twenty-years hence with twenty-thousand striving day by day
Shah Jahan had her lasting monument—the Taj Mahal
Where millions could honour Mumtaz, stand in awe, and pray.
In this fairy-like palace towering over all,

In white marble symbolic of love and purity,
The shimmering domes like rounded clouds seem to float in air
Above the river blessed by the magic company
Of this enchanted castle; in this world there is nought so fair.

As the Taj expands above and beyond—love, beauty, death,
And peacefulness seems close together in this hallowed ground;
Where aromatic perfume of flowers fills every breath
And silky saris in reds, blues, silver and gold astound.

Behold the white marble mausoleum stunning in the sun;
The dome like a breast full of milk stands for the vault of heaven;
The square of this creation for the worldly realm of all and one;
Symbolically uniting heaven and earth till amen.

On the queen's sepulchre the design of a slate is seen
And on the emperor's an ink well—"The king writes
The desires of his soul on the heart of a queen
To obey in heaven as she had on Earth all days and nights."

But his fate was to be a prisoner at Agra Fort;
Dethroned by Aurangzeb his son; longingly he gazed
Across the river to her sarcophagus—Oh! a life too short—
Too short; day after day he gazed until nearly crazed.

"If on earth there be a paradise of bliss, it is this,
It is this." See these words in the Agra Fort's great hall.
To Shah Jahan paradise on Earth was her queenly kiss
And for his last nine years his sole thought was Mumtaz Mahal.

We leave behind the two false tombs and crypts below;
The flute that will not die within the reverberating dome,
The precious stones, peace, and beauty all around. Now we know
Justice cannot be done in sprightly poem or mighty tome.

Now as silent night creeps in—its mystic veil comes too soon;
The sky powdered in soft white stars holds sovereignty
Over the main dome mysterious and bright as a full moon;
Over the guardian twin mosques in all their divinity;

Over the daughter domes, and the four towering sons.
Below—bazaars sparkle like little stars in the gloom;
And the Jumna River like a silver strand lazily runs
As centuries before—while our hearts return to the tomb.

Lovers Come and Lovers Go

Prompted by a comment from long-time friend and poet Wayne Cosgrove, "Lovers come and lovers go, but friendship goes on forever."

Lovers come and lovers go;
You feel bad when you're apart;
They hurt you when they depart.
Is it worth it—I think so.

Love is a beautiful thing
I'll grant you this my friend,
But it will get you in the end.
Bite the apple and feel the sting.

Sex is but a fleeting thing;
It starts as a simple fling,
But then it's gone on the wing.
Yes sex has a hollow ring.

Lovers burn out all too soon;
They will not last many a moon.
But without the sex friendship stays
Through bright and bitter days.

A Kiss Is Not a Kiss Anymore

We came a long way together—
Many years, tears and laughter.
How I yearn for yesteryear:
Days of love, wine and cheer.

Amongst my faded souvenirs—
Are these never dying memories.
How did it all come down to this?
Where his kiss is no longer a kiss.

Slowly his passion went somewhere—
Appearing with his silver hair.
Now his love is but a dying ember,
Yet the burning flame I still remember.

I still long for his loving touch,
But holding hands is just too much.
He'll always be the one I adore,
But a kiss is not a kiss anymore.

Whispering Winds

In your silent moments think of me when:
The soft rain of summer will fall—
Bringing sweet memories of you and me;
The golden autumn re-awakens the soul;
The winter blast rekindles our warm kiss of bliss;
Each spring brings life anew;
And always when the winds will blow—
Whispering—I love you, I love you—
On low, a gentle love,
On high, a passionate love.

Never Over You

Getting over you, is hard to do.
My heart must have its say,
And tears gets in my way.
No matter how I try,
The memories will not die,
They seem like yesterday.
When friends ask of you, I can only lie;
If only they'd stop asking about you.
"Nearly over you,"—is never true.
Getting over you, is hard to do.

Lost Love

Beside the black and orange of a flickering campfire
in darkest Africa—
I picture you like a flame appearing and reappearing.
I'm hoping your thoughts are flickering too—
Back to the happy moments together.
Too quick they came and went,
But like undying embers
They still will burn—on and on . . .

You and I

For many blissful years there was just you and I
Together we hoped for ever and ever.
Many the secrets we shared just you and I;
Laughing, loving and living each hour together;
But too good to last those days of you and I.

The Spring in My Life

It was spring, spring, spring—
The hot sun embracing the skin—
Freshness and energy
Recharging the air.
In the cool woods,
Trilliums, trilliums everywhere
On the forest floor;
All with heads bowed—
In thankful prayer for their new born life.
Likewise I give thanks,
For spring reminds me of you:
    the beauty,
    the vitality,
    and vivacity.
You are the spring in my steps;
You are the spring in my life.

We Love To Go A-Wandering

We love to go a-wandering on trails serene:
Where nature abounds all around;
Where cares take flight and float away . . .
In heady air to a happy sky.
The forest has many regal faces reminding of:
The spring: a new born baby fresh and eager for life;
The summer: a young princess dancing in garb of green;
The fall: a stately prince parading in multi-coloured robes;
The winter: a king sometimes harsh but sometimes sprightly
With ever flowing white beard.

Today though the fall has nearly died—the woods are still alive
Passing their energy to our band of three.
It's tempting to linger here and there—
At each sparkling stream or lookout supreme
As we marvel at each bend and rise of the trail,
And stand and stare—drinking in the wonder of it all . . ..
But then, feet are eager to fly once more o'er the ground.
At days end—spent and reluctant we depart our forest friend.

Decades later when the trail becomes too rugged and long,
Our memories will linger there . . . and relive each step . . .
Those joyful hours of wandering and wondering . . .

Sweet Memories Exceed Painful Longing

He could picture himself strolling
As if in a dream—
On some solitary beach—
With the surging surf by his side.
Now he was old—too old.
On this gray day he had only memories of her:
When he felt young and vibrant in heart
Because of her;
When he was in love with her,
Lost in love with her;
When life was heaven but he didn't know it then;
It was bitter sweet to think on this yesteryear
This lost love. She was gone but still here.
The many many happy times together
Were with him forever
And kept repeating, repeating,
Like the returning waves—
Days of singing body,
dancing mind,
and laughing spirit.
He could picture her face lit up with love.
These longing but sweet memories filled his empty heart
In his lonely walk by the ocean so unconsoling,
With millions of tears of its own;
No trees to embrace him in his melancholy;
No sun to offer warm consolation;
And only the wind for a dumb companion,
To remind how he loved the wind in her hair.

But finally, the sun burst out scattering silver into the waves,
And he began to realize:
These sweet memories exceed the painful longing—
And what a wasted life if she had not been there.

LAUGH

The Party

It was a party to end all parties,
Back in forty-nine in dear old Ireland,
A birthday bash for Uncle Ned to please;
Twenty of us happy and a four-piece band,
O'Reilly on the banjo, Mike on the flute
Sonny on the fiddle, and Sal on the uke.

We filled cousin Clancy's cottage to the brim
With smoke and laughter and plenty of vim;
Outside the soft, silent rain was a falling—
A white column of smoke slowly a rising
To the stars above the silver ground,
And the revelry could be heard for miles around.

The evening wore on past the moonlit night—
And the chilly morn recalled quite a sight:
The jugs were near empty; the feet sore
From jigging, and the band could play no more;
Two jugs of whiskey sadly smashed, one broken toe;
Twenty fuzzy heads coming in the morrow;
Clancy caught his girl kissing a beau;
Two strings busted on the old banjo;
Uncle Ned on his peg leg out danced them all,
Then! finally collapsed like a domino.
Now when the fire died, they feared the end of the ball;
Without peat it was bound for defeat, so it was agreed—
Only one solution or we must retire:
Throw! Uncle Ned's wooden leg on the fire.

Philosophy in a Nutshell

Having a problem—no matter	*Here's the solution:*
Feeling unloved:	*Get a dog.*
Giving a word to the wise:	*Useless—required only for the stupid.*
How to look better:	*For some women—wear as little as possible.*
Not wealthy:	*Count blessings, for example, if healthy feel rich.*
Feeling old:	*Think young! Act young!*
Feeling useless:	*Wake up! It's probably true.*
Life sucks:	*But beats "no life" every time.*
Decide right:	*Right decision if it "just feels right" Think with open heart.*
Cannot solve difficult problem:	*Be patient—some things often resolve themselves.*
Solve difficult situation:	*A little fib can sometimes be quite useful.*
Feeling blue:	*Give someone a hug. Smile—pass it on.*
Need help:	*If someone too eager to help—run.*
Failing a lot lately:	*Live up to it! Failure may be your thing.*
How to become a good conversationalist:	*Concentrate on "you" not "I."*
Indecision at fork in road:	*Take it!*
Before agreeing or disagreeing:	*Ask yourself WIFME? "(What's in it for me?)*
Life is humdrum:	*Wake up! Put some life into your life. Live with a passion.*

Doggon Dog Story

I swear this is the most doggon true dog story I ever heerd:
It seems out in Saskatchewan there was happenin's weird.
Of course we Easterners aren't supprised of what comes
out of the West,
Though we ponder the East- West sitiation it always puts
our mind to the test.
Oh yes, back to the dog story.
I have not rightly fixed my mind whether this little pooch was the smartest
In the world, or with the dumbest owners, but maybe just blessed,
For he was run over by the owners auto—ah cruel fate.
Now with no breath or heartbeat he was surely at the pearly gate;
So sadly they buried him two feet under in the back yard;
But Eureka! one day later he comes in lookin' for his pard.
Doggon!
Now he keeps lookin' 'round suspicious like with only one eye;
Yes distrustful like—I ask you—wouldn't you and I?

Race to the Whirlpool Favourite Spot

Laboriously dragging his feet—
the crippled young man with the cane
approaches the whirlpool;
The last 10 meters had taken two minutes or more it seems.
He's relishing the thought of the warmth on his aching legs.
Bannister ran the four minute mile
in the time my young friend would take
to reach the whirlpool from 20 meters away
to his favourite spot
and my favourite spot too
in the north east corner of the whirlpool,
where the powerful jets prevail.
I can see the deep concentration—his eyes are glued on that spot;
He's been thinking about it all the painful day.
I'm already steaming away in the whirlpool
but not in our favourite spot.
The devil in me says, "Just when he is two meters away . . . dash into our favourite spot,"
just to see the disappointment in his eyes,
just as in my youthful years when we
watched the elderly
slowly approach the open elevator—
suddenly! we closed the doors in their faces.
What fun!
In my 68th year I'm feeling young and adventurous again with this fiendish plot.
Finally, he's only three meters away—
I've got to act fast.

I couldn't do it this time—the angels prevailed.
Little did he know the evil I had been thinking.
We smile at each other as usual as he eventually
Sinks down . . .
in our favourite spot . . .
feeling the warmth like a Mother's womb . . .
while the life drifts back into his young but old legs,
And I smile within.

Lucky Out of Love

I searched and searched many a dreary hall of dance
Hoping by some quirk of chance to find romance,
But fortunate was I
For no one caught my eye.

My next thought was to advertise
For someone voluptuous but wise;
Once again Lady Luck smiled on me
For I found most seemed far too wise about my money.

Last week I had a very close call
When for a classy lass I did fall;
In a moment of weakness I proposed—for she was a rare find;
T'was a narrow escape believe me—when she politely declined.

Countless hours I've pondered and wondered why,
While thousands of blank faces passed me by.
It's perplexing and vexing why nothing connects,
But fortune beamed since after all—most were rejects.

Now with priorities straight I'm saving time,
Getting fitter, smarter and the freedom is sublime.
Someone surely is looking after me from above,
It's my only explanation for being lucky out of love.

CANADA
86
WORLD MASTERS ATHLETICS CHAMPIONSHIPS

Old Suckers Never Stop

"Just look at that old sucker go!"
marvelled the students as I propelled
my near sixty-five year old bones across the finish line
on the desert dry indoor track at York U.
I had just used up three-hundred metres of my life
in a stressful forty-four seconds,
even beating one of these teenagers who had not yet
discovered the secret of Dedication.
But surprisingly to those that marvelled:
there was no collapse—like a house made of cards;
the Red Cross did not rush up with oxygen;
and somehow the stretcher bearers were not required.
Then they saw some twenty pounds of lard
was missing from my bones,
and a look of steely Confidence in the eye was there
born from thousands of hours of playing with my pals:
Speedy, Mighty, Hearty, and Persy (for Perseverance).
I plan to continue to "go like an old sucker"
until The Ultimate Meet Director stops me in my tracks,
after about ten times more around the globe—I reckon.

Once In a Lovetime

It could take years to happen, yes sirree,
That once in a lifetime, once in a lovetime mate
Who satisfies all your dreams unexpectedly
And your weary search is over—ah lucky fate.

But then metamorphosis sets in and hubby shows decline:
Your Robert Redford now is as sexy as Groucho Marx;
Your Einstein now has the smarts of Frankenstein;
And your once in a lovetime flame no longer sparks.

Your Abe Lincoln now is as crooked as a used car salesman;
Your Roger Dangerfield now is as funny as Boris Karloff;
Your Swarzenager now is as fit as the circus fat man;
And the once in a love time mirage is over and off.

At first it was but a subtle nasal sound,
But as years passed it changed to a sick lawn mower,
Then to a chain saw rattle that shook the walls around,
So goodbye Carl with your schnozzola of one hundred horsepower.

O' Reilly lost his zest and nothing he would do,
But sit with the TV converter in his right
And a beer in his left while to the tube he did glue,
But when the tube blew he blew too—one hockey night.

For Walter it wasn't the underwear strewn everywhere,
Or the wandering eyes for the fair maidens he saw,
Or betting the nags, or the way he did swear,
But the toilet seat left up—was the last straw.

For Eric it all boiled down to the way he chewed each vittle;
At mealtime—over his giant mouthfuls she did stew;
So farewell brother, your chawing bothered more than a little;
Once too oft you bit off more than you could chew.

Louiji claimed to drink very little, but it was far too often
To suit the wifey, "This sipa, sipa, all day long has to stop
For your liver will do you in lest you have forgotten."
But the day that he did stop was the day he did drop.

Albert had a passion for cats, not one but more than a few;
First there was Felix, Sweety, Penelopy, and Calamity;
When the number grew to twenty-two—wifey knew not what to do;
She only knew she was involved in a categorical catastrophe.

So beware the annoying habit and to your spouse attend,
For all are not blessed with patience eternal;
May the good habit of restraint be your friend,
Otherwise, a sweet spouse can be a femme fatale infernal.

Bad Hair Expressions

Some expressions are too much too bare:
"Bad hair day," is one I declare.
What's the worry, no need for chagrin:
A bad cut will grow back in agin.

Some gals say I'm lookin' for a "Hunk,"
Presumably one to match the clunk
In their head. If it's flesh alone—
It's sure to wind up as a groan.

Now we come to "It's all relative."
To what, your mother- in- law or a sieve?
This always leaves me dumfounded,
In wonderment and scratching my head.

Then the ultimate, "Done that, been there."
These braggarts take notice and beware:
Next time I hear it I'll render
A chop in the jaw for a reminder.

The other extreme is no expression:
You crave for a grain of compassion,
But sadly in return is the wall;
It's no ball tennis or just aerosol.

Blast the "four fingered quotation marks:"
In conversation this really narks,
Somehow it's just not natural;
Next time I see it foretells fatale.

The teenager's favorite word is "stuff."
To come up with the right word is tough,
But when all things are made of stuff—
I say really—enough is enough.

Sadly there are many a cliché
Such as nice, like, bling, whatever, gay,
It's not rocket science, or brain surgery,
Me bad, there you go, and absolutely.
Let us wipe out all this tomfoolery.

Calling All Big Sisters

I searched and searched for the perfect mate
In many a hall of dance till hours late
And here and there and everywhere
For someone wise and beauteous fair.
Now it's all too clear—sights were too high
And now still lonely I'm left with but a sigh.
But listen—here comes the real twister:
I realize now what I need is a Big Sister,
One who worries not that I am a mister,
One just to talk to, with just a hug when blue,
And one who cares not if I am not a who's who.
Then after some months with my Big Sister
Maybe, she won't mind if I kissed her.

Limericks

A bachelor grey had a great dread
Of his possible prowess in bed.
A lovely one he did know,
But he proposed even so.
'Twas a narrow scrape—she nearly accepted.

Carl wished for a wife with a name with erotica;
He pondered on Virginia, Lovalota,
And even Ophelia;
It was a real phobia.
Sadly in the end he had to wed Agatha.

A city housewife was stressed and hyper;
Hubby agreed she needed a helper;
Being modern, a robot
Was selected and bought.
But it couldn't even change a diaper.

The Humane Society is bungling
On a catastrophe quite troubling;
It's the fiasco
Down in Mexico;
They're still unable to stop the cat juggling.

A bachelor tried 'Dial a Belle Bride'
And engaged before he spied.
Alas, things looked better over the phone.
He remained glum and alone,
For the females he met were as cold as stone.

McTavish drove his wife round the bendo;
His weakness was a wee game of Nontendo.
All day the bleep, bleep, bleep,
Then played it in his sleep
Till the wife screamed, "Nay more, or leave
I intendo!"

Elmer had a boring nocturnal habit;
His nasal roar bothered the wife quite a bit;
Since it resembled a sick chain saw
She thought, "It should be agin' the law,
This schnozzola will surely make me git."

O'Reilly lost his zest and naught he would do,
Except to the TV he was ever true,
With converter in his right
And a beer all day and night,
But sadly, when the boob tube blew he blew too.

Cathy had a passion for cats too many;
Firstly there was only Penelopy,
But hubby knew not what to do
When the number reached twenty-two;
He only knew it was a Catastrophe.

A perpetual peeper was caught peeping
When a tree branch broke while some nudes
he was seeking,
"Your Honor, It's not that I am too loose
To the Judge he had the most lame excuse:
It's only logical—I was born in Peeking."

A regurgitator practiced till his throat was sore
With billiard balls, keys and articles galore;
Big or small he'd give it a try.
When others said, "This could make you die,"
He'd always reply, "Why do you bring this up."

Max searched for an independent lass 'till one day
He discovered Fay who liked to do things her "vay."
Then happy was he, so they did marry.
But too late he learned it must be her "vay"
or no way.

Count Drac's Last Party

In the world of monsters and witches they're talking still
Of Count Drac's party in his castle
In Transylvania way back in fourteen-ninety:
a monstrous, ghoulish,
devilish, bewitching party.
Centuries later the villagers nearby
spoke of that morn
of weird happenings
stranger than strange itself!

The moon was full that dreadful night
Bathing the castle in shining white
While Death gazed down from on high,
Down from the towers of Dracula.
High up on the mountain it did loom.
They came silently by stealth . . .
In the gloom and in the dead of night—
To his party to relive and devour
at his castle of doom.
Arriving by curse and by horse-drawn hearse
from the tombs of Egypt,
from the graveyards and many a crypt,
and from Hell and beyond—
All dying to attend.
Many an unsavoury monster trudged . . .
the winding road upwards
Through a fog so thick you could bite it—
But no—not a fog, just a dozen or so ghost
Floating onwards to meet the not so gracious host.
At the door of the moat he did gloat;
Many a dirty trick he'd planned:
several trap door and heinous acts galore.

The cooks flew in—ten witches cackling
Soon to gather round a boiling vat;
The fire from the pot casting huge flickering shadows
on the damp stone walls.
Into the vat gleefully they mixed:
gizzard of the goat,
liver of the toad,
fang of the serpent,
and veins from everywhere.
The Devil and thirteen demons and other unwanted guests
Dropped in!
One demon promptly lost his tail in the witches brew;
A similar fate befell the headless monster
who arrived with head under his arm;
He'd carelessly laid it down—
thinking no harm—
into the pot it went.
A big hit with the guests were the bloody Dracs,
the Count's favourite drink,
Quite a few beforehand he'd quaffed no doubt.
The pickled kid's feet were also a particular treat.
But all wondered and feared what was to be the main course;
With chagrin they learned this was left to Frankenstein.

As the morn wore on the gracious host tried
to kiss each guest,
But they wanted none of it not even in jest
For they knew of his problem of 'bloodfromallism'.
Sadly, as a host he was quite a dud
For all he wanted from each was blood.
With great pride he displayed his trophies:
wind chimes of human bones,
drums of human skin with tibia bone sticks,
necklaces of human digits bleached white in the sun,
and the skull candle stick holders throughout the great hall.

Ah! what a night of revelry:
The Count wished to dance cheek to cheek with anyone
male or female,
But only the mummies agreed for blood they had none;
One became quite unravelled, to annoyance and grim amusement of all
And tripped up quite a few in reams of mouldy cloth;
The frog monster hit the chandeliers again and again
with his aerial hops during the polka.
While the wolf man with hair down to his feet
tripped self and others too, too often.
While most found difficulty keeping time
with the doleful organ music.

The fiendish sounds filled the valleys—
reached the village below,
and mountains afar.
Listen!
the cackling of the witches,
the organ music so ponderous and funereal,
the screams and moans,
for it was forbotten to laugh.
The guests began to wonder about the Devil?
Was it male or female or both?
They were eager to tear off the Devils clothing .
to find out,
For by now the demons had quite a few bloody Dracs
and some demons had gone mysteriously missing,
When Frankenstein arrived with the main course:
two scrawny teenagers under one arm
and an old geezer under the other.
This threw the guests into an uproar:
One and all complained of the fare.
Sad it was to see one of such bulk
Weeping in a corner where he did sulk.

But then the method of cooking was up for debate:
Finally after much argument,
the young ones were for barbecue,
the tough old one for stew in witches brew.

The morning moaned on and the guests screamed on:
Now the wind chimes and organ were sounding mighty low
It looked like maybe time to go.
The Count by now had far too many of the bloody Dracs-
Even the witches were looking good.
In a bold move, desperate for a dancing mate
He grabbed Frankenstein for a spin,
Putting the giant into a rage.
Just then shimmers of dawn were shattering the blackness—
The Count flew into a frenzy:
tipped over the witches brew—boiling many feet,
tore down the wind chimes,
pushed three mummies and a witch over the castle wall,
threw a demon over by the tail,
and smashed the organ—
its last ominous groan lingering
briefly in the misty mountain air.
Alas! all good things must come to an end.

In the village below a late carouser
wearily greeting the dawn
wondered on the sudden silence from the castle,
Looking up he saw a series of white cloud like puffs of smoke
rapidly exiting from the castle,
but rising much faster than smoke,
And perhaps ten or so huge black objects much larger than crows
also exiting from the top of the castle.
Then his ears were overwhelmed by:
pounding of hoofs, rattling harness,
and churning of wheels on stone and hard earth.

Suddenly! he had to jump clear as a multitude of hearses
Shot by, charging, careening, churning up the road—
As if chased by the Devil or worse!
Strangely all without drivers except the last hearse
There sat a driver—headless.
The horses appeared to have fire from the nostrils
so he thought.
And following behind this procession
it seemed like twenty feet on each bound . . .
a strange frog-like man, with croaking sounds.
The whirl of the speeding wheels soon faded in the distance
leaving behind clouds of dust
and strangely strewn about great lengths of mouldy cloth.

When the cock crowed in the morn and the village awoke—
The mouldy cloth had blown away,
And no villager noticed on the road
the huge web shaped foot prints,
the size of a pail.
The frantic tale of these weird sights and sounds from our lone reveller
only cast suspicion on his sanity,
which he questioned himself.
Many a villager was convinced his meanderings were simply
a nightmare brought on by a batch of bad alcohol.
Sadly he developed twitch of the eyeball,
And never again did he imbibe.

But it has been rumored now for six centuries:
that a monster named Frankenstein
had choked the blood out of Count Dracula
that very morn.
So the story goes in Transylvania

Let Us

Let us give thanks to Leonard Cohen
for this basic idea of "let us"
Not lettuce—this is not a salad,
` *but maybe a salad of life.*

Let us not waste time in making it rhyme—
It's for the bygone time;
Unlike dancing—you don't have to be in
Step.

Let us not call the Quebecers "Whiners,"
Let us not call them winers,
After all there is nothing so bad as a "whining winer".

Let us not investigate the sex life of presidents:
Every hubby should have a hobby.

Let us discourage the snowboarders from smoking pot:
A joint is not worth a broken joint.

Let us stop this chasing the opposite sex
All this wasted time, energy, and money too;
Let us have a pill to quell all this madness.

Let us not ask our lady friends to see our etchings:
Let us be more truthful.

Let us speak Chrétienese—the Jeanne Chrétien kind,
Let us loosen up and have some fun:
For example, "He was not heavy because he was light."
However, Jeanne, please no more throttling.

Let us have someone to love us to death,
Someone to welcome us home with enthusiasm,
Someone who makes you the only one in their life—a dog.

Let us stop chasing money, money, and material things:
Don't try to keep up with the Jones'
Just try to keep up with yourself.

Let us give thanks to the lovers that never were
Chances are they would have been a burr
Under the saddle, in the end.

Let us die young, with a sense of humor,
But live for a century.

PATHOS

No More No More

Casey House (Toronto home for the terminal)
May 1994

God bless you—we love you.
Did he hear? I pray he did;
His lips moved a moment as if in reply.
My mind keeps drifting back to those painful days:
Hard to believe this was my proud brother
Once so handsome, so independent,
Walking tall about the world;
And now decaying fast . . .
With spotted flesh wasting away
Revealing bone and dark hollow eyes;
And with dazed mind—
Already half in another world;
And now too proud to be seen by others,
Except by me his closest kIn.

Two short months before the end by some miracle
With my meagre help he dragged his frame—
From bed to lawyer and downtown clinic
For one last visit;
Pathetically losing his pants due to lost flesh;
Courageously stating to the counsellor—
Who offered a book Living With Death—
He knew all about living with Death.
Even the other fearful patients could tell his time was nigh;
Their young faces told too well of a similar fate.

In my daily visits the words came hard.
We could have talked of happy youthful days,
But we talked of "the arrangements" left to me.
I had thoughts only of his artistic past,
His courage, and his full though shortened life.
Now the words unsaid come easy—years later—
But too late, too late.

Wasting away hour by hour as if in starvation
On an express ride to another world;
There's no return it's plain;
Death is the determined driver
Not to be deterred—it was waiting in his room.
This ride's going to be a short one
Charging through the dark tortured haze
At a faster and faster rate.

Then he had only his dreams;
Or was it nightmares?
I hope he dreamt of happy young days
Before life became grim;
Perhaps remembering
Running and hiding in yellow corn fields
In the summer sun with his brothers,
Or recalling not so happy poor times,
The character building days,
When we went reluctantly—

Door to door trying to sell mama's donuts,
Or collecting solitary chunks of coal at the railroad tracks,
And the embarrassment of wearing welfare clothes to school.
But I hope at the last—hearing from yesteryear
The peaceful strains of violins
And the laughter of loved ones.
And as his mind drifted in the pain, perhaps wandering . . .
Back again to exotic lands visited and late friends of all races
Thousands of miles away;
Thinking in his delirium—will they sometimes
Wonder about his whereabouts and his silence . . ..

Then the morphine was given
To ease the transition to the forever land—
His last journey.
No more to hear the morning chorus of joyous birds;
No more the thrill of freshness of spring;
No more to be caught up with white clouds
Racing on a hot ocean day;
No more the feeling of awe on a still starry night
With white stars as countless as drops of rain;
No more the touch and sound of loved ones;
No more the feel of warm soft rain
On once young vibrant skin;
No more, no more, no more.

Bird in the House

-Based on a true incident in Rosedale, Yonge Street,
Toronto in April 1991.
Truth is stranger than fiction.

"A wild bird inside a house portends death," so they say;
When first I heard this superstition so sad,
My mind raced back to decades ago
To the crowded Greek restaurant in Rosedale, Toronto,
Where the tiny bird darted in from the hot summer street
Into the cool semi gloom—
Smashing itself on the wall above—
And falling limply on my ailing brother's empty plate.
At sixty-four many other unaccountable events had happened
To him, a poetic wanderer of the globe.
Now life was but an aimless journey of pain unending.
Had he known this he would have rejoiced, perhaps,
Since death was his daily wish—
And death was his constant companion
Riding on his shoulder.
This hapless foul incident marked the last meal with dear brother Maurice;
Sadly, I sensed he had lost taste for food and life.
A few months later the superstition rang true!
Strange how the bird knew its destination in its final flight;
Picking my brother out in the over-crowded restaurant,
Strange that it knew the superstition too.

I'll Be Home for Christmas

The imagined last words of dear Aunt Bertha, December 1999

"Ninety-four years filled with work, work, joy and loved ones;
Now there's only pain, tears and strangers;
Ninety-four but it seems like forty-four.
I'll be leaving Detroit soon:
This boom box black and white city
of cars and broken dreams.
Seems like yesterday on the farm
with sisters Lola, Alice, and Della;
The prairie got in my blood,
The endless sky over a sleeping giant with the golden flowing hair.
How we loved our mares and stallions:
Laxie, Goldie, Maxie and good old Jake."
—"I'm riding my pony Lucky in the sun once again:
Feeling free and fast as the wind;
Come Lola I'll race you back to the barn . . .
—Della and Alice come look at the fireworks
One-hundred miles away—that's Saskatoon Exhibition . . .
—Papa's been gone too long from town:
It's a blinding snow storm—
Mama keeps looking out the window,
but there's nothing to see;
When fear sets in—the wind whistles and wails
right inside the heart . . .
—It's forty below and we're stranded in our sleigh caboose the six of us;
Thank goodness for the hot rocks at our feet;
The horses are exhausted after plunging through the snow up to their bellies;

Now they can move no further . . .
—Its spring, glorious spring!
Look Mama three new born calves;
Papa will be pleased . . .
—It's fall and I'm helping Mama in the kitchen
at threshing time;
We seem to be cooking and baking all day and night;
But look at the satisfaction on their hungry faces . . .
—But they're all gone now:
The animals, the threshing crew, Mama, Papa, and two dear sisters;
And I pray I'll be with them soon."
"My eyesight is bad too:
My strange helpers only a blur, moving in a fog;
They speak so soft and low to me,
Why can't I hear?
Feelin' weaker every day.
The high walls of this bed are a jail to me—
Like a children's crib.
I feel like a child again with diapers and all.
If only the Lord would take me in his arms
to erase this pain and tears.
Christmas is around the corner I think—
My last one for sure, but—
I'll be home for Christmas"

Tsunami

Before

They rose to another idyllic fresh new dawn—souls singing—,
Another silent awakening
Except for the murmuring waves with its incessant lazy tide
And soft fragrant breezes rustling the palms.
Colorful fishing boats rocking gently cast shadows on the benevolent blue sea
Sparkling this morning.
Most natives taking it all for granted—just another day of sand, sea and golden sun.
But truly they loved their life by the sea:
Eking out a living by the relentless sea.
But today would be a day to remember for all time:
Sunday, December twenty-six, two-thousand and four.

During

"We're going to the beach with our parents to see the huge waves."
"Hurry—come along."
Thousands of innocents, natives and tourists, but mostly children flocked to the beaches—
Mystified—and oblivious of the danger
Even though many had sensed the shaking ground that morning.
Today the deep blue ocean they loved was acting mighty strange.
It rose up then receded—scraping the sea bed dry behind it—
Advancing and retreating several times revealing:
colorful shells, floundering fish, and rock and reef formations.

What fun!"
Oh! See the monstrous waves crashing and spraying.
Oh! See the hidden reefs and all these treasures.
But Death was lurking and advancing with fast waves—
Waves a kilometer away now looked ominous—
Rapidly growing in size—
Gigantic white thoroughbreds speeding to shore
Faster than a jet plane at 800 km/hour.
This time the ocean rose up and raced far up the beeches to new territory—the homes and roads.
Tsunami had arrived—the most devastating on record.

Some Teutonic plates ten kilometers below the sea bed
And thousands of miles long had moved from East and West and opposed each other—
Creating gigantic pressures.
Something had to give:
An Earthquake the largest in 40 years triggered
And rocked the Indian Ocean
Causing the ocean depths to move immediately East and West
At six to eight miles per minute towards the shores of a dozen countries
Some 3000 miles away—
A force equal to over 20 atomic bombs,
Or more treacherous than a thousand sea monsters.
In a few hours millions would be homeless
All from a few millimeters of movement miles below the sea bed.
On reaching the thousands of shores it was:
"Run for your life to higher ground!"
But too late.

On reaching land the wall of water encountering friction—slowed—but rose—
On some beaches some walls of death:
as high as a man,
some three stories high,
and even thirty meters high.
The unforgiving sea came speeding to shore:
A battering ram, devouring all in its path;
Man-made structures mere match sticks in this torrent.
And impossible to outrun a wall of black water and debris at locomotive speed.

It sounded like the end of the world:
Starting with a high pitched wail followed by
a hoarse maddening,
ever increasing,
near deafening roar—
Like a hurricane or a nearby speeding freight train,
Mingled with a thousand screams,
And the twang and crash of shattering structures:
crunching wood,
tearing of tin roofs.
Striking terror into hearts threatening to escape the chest.
Waves of death eager to reach the shore:
Exploding beach homes,
Crushing boats like tin cans,
Crumpling tin roofs like sheets of paper,
Uprooting trees,
Moving boulders as big as a car,
Filling hotel rooms to the ceiling,
Sluicing some tourists out windows, trapping others inside,
Creating battling-ram strong winds,
Twisting iron rails into pretzel shapes,
Overturning and flooding trains,

Wiping out entire villages and occupants,
Submerging some low islands completely,
Turning streets into rivers of debris from wrecked homes.
In its maddening rush carrying building materials, furniture,
overturned cars, buses, and bodies for blocks
before receding at the same terrific speed;
Sweeping dead and alive thousands of meters out to sea.
Then returning again and again.
"Here it comes again!"
For several hours the waves:
Racked the shores,
Lashed the shores,
Pummeled the shores.
For millions it felt like the end of the world
And for 160,000 to 200,000 it was—
Instantaneous burial,
On thousands of miles of beaches and seaside communities.

The tsunami death bell was ringing
Far and wide.
Death followed the waves to and from shore stalking—
The thousands of beaches for thousands of miles around,
To explode—on the shore,
To release pent up, boundless energies,
Undiminished after thousands of miles.
It was harrowing hours of Hell on Earth.

Aftermath

In the days after—the waves were once again whispering low and soft . . .
A tired repentant sea at peace,
But the roar of nature—a symphony like a thousand angry lions ever increasing—
Intermingled with thousands of screams
Piercing the air—
Will remain with the survivors forever.
And for millions there's nothing left but the memories.

For the fortunate survivors their nightmare on these many paradise islands was over.
Intact families still living rose at dawn—feeling the lingering sadness—
But feeling more alive from a great gratitude on surviving a disaster.

The beaming sun rises each sprightly dawn out of the sea turning the sea to a golden red—
Seeking to apply soothing balm to the remaining living.
But their lands are now a sea of devastation:
The bodies, the clutter—the debris everywhere—demoralizing,
Bodies stacked like cordwood high in neat piles,
The smell of rotting flesh, human and livestock,
The living wander about disillusioned—looking for missing family,
The pictures of the previous morn keep flashing in troubled minds,
Thousands of lifeless lay by the roadside for pickup,
Some still slumped high up in trees,
Some impaled on fences,
Bloated bodies floating like dead fish,
All to go in mass graves,
Wandering orphans by the thousands,
Wrecked boats piled into small mountains by these horrific tides,
And millions of disillusioned homeless in makeshift tents.
These scenes too typical of the aftermath.

But as in all disasters there were miracles:

A man survives for two weeks adrift on a raft—initially caught in a ten meter wave,
"feeling like trapped in a giant washing machine;"
A man lives for eight days clinging to a palm tree;
An elephant plucks a human from the raging ocean;
A dog pulls a seven-year old to safety of a hill;
A father saves self, wife and two sons by tying all to a tree with beach towels;
Wild animals and aborigine tribes sensed the disaster and moved safely to higher ground,
saved by an extensive, reliable warning system—the birds;
Children carried miles away by the tidal wave reunited with families;
A twenty-day old baby survives on a mattress;
A four-year old boy stranded in a tree for nearly three days without food or water;
A six-year old girl survives clinging to a sofa cushion;
An eight-year old boy wakes up in a mass grave—just before burial time;
A mother gives birth in a forest during the catastrophe—they call the boy Tsunami.

Faith is shaken—
But knowing the infinite and God's way are difficult to comprehend, they continue to pray.
But for many, they have only their prayers since left with:
Shattered homes,
Shattered livelihood,
Shattered souls and spirit,
But most of all thoughts of loved ones washed away.

Still the stars will shine and the sun will beam on this sea and lands.
Fisherman longing to build boats and repair nets will return once more to haul in their harvest with knotted, tanned hands from the fickle sea.
All will be forgiven to this benevolent but sometimes angry friend.
And the people will return to live beside the sea.

Around the world their cry was heard from their far-away once idyllic lands.
A hundred years from now or two-hundred years from now they will speak of this tsunami of all tsunami's—
The granddaddy of all tsunami's.
Producing a world generosity never before paralleled.
Truly a day to remember for all time.

Fear

Based on a realistic WW2 dream

It was the silent dawn in England
The day that struck fear
like an icicle into his heart—had come.
A grey misty morning but still the birds were singing
Reminding him of happy times,
But there was no way out—a secret solo flying mission
To bomb a factory in Dusseldorf.
He had known sickly fear in his earlier teens—before the steeplechase,
But now he knew that was not real fear.
What he felt now was a hundred fold greater.
He felt not an ounce of courage—
"If only there were others with me."
His superior officer explained the details . . .
His words were as if from a different world weirdly strange and muffled.
The young pilot heard only deadly fear—
Saw only doom—
Sensed only death—
Felt trapped.
But there was no way out.
With confident air—oblivious to his pilot's inner despair
His superior talked of the return journey.
Crossing the Rhine and straight home.
"Why did I join? Why me? I'm only twenty-one!" he thought.
Certain was he there would be no return—
No return.
It all seemed a colossal mistake, to die alone.
"If only there were others with me.
If only my friend Jake was with me."
He was walking to the gallows for sure,
Fear—it pounded his heart,
Fear—it churned his stomach,
Fear—it enveloped his every cell.
The roar of the plane filled his ears, but he heard only fear.
If only there was one last time at the Squirrel and Lion,
one last time to hold Yvette,
one last time to say goodbye to Mom.
Then he was heaven bound—
Leaving the earth behind—
Enveloped in the bosom of the clouds
He thought, "It's just you and me now Lord, and my prayers,"
But suddenly, he was calm . . .
And he knew he was no longer alone.

Ride With the Valkyries

Inspired by Scandinavian friend Chris Erickson

Olaf stood proud behind the sea serpent prow
of his great longship
Taking pride in the speed of his sleek ship—
His bronze twenty-stone frame glistened in the
silvery spray
As the ship, twenty-four meters long, sliced
the white laced waves.
His brave warriors eighty strong:
young adventurers,
robust farmers,
and seasoned warriors;
Felt luck (prized more than courage) to serve
under their fearsome captain,
And felt safe with the 20 longships behind—
Pushed by the God of Wind.
For many moons the sky was their tent,
The shimmering stars their silent solace,
Their shield their hard bed,
Their sword and spear their faithful friend.
In their pagan thoughts and dreams were:
Maidens with fulsome hips and breasts,
Goblets of mead in silver horns,
Female slaves serving foods aplenty,
Feuds at feast time,
Boastings of heroic deeds and past victories,
And the Valkyries: voluptuous maidens
serving brave warriors in Valhalla.

Every day roaming the seas—
Free as a hawk in a universe of sky.
Again and again to hit and run swift as an eagle
after innocent prey,
But perchance to hear the Valkyries magic song.
On many a day another Viking adventure:
Plunderings, and burnings,
A life of fire, blood and battle,
The reddening of spears, swords and battle axe
in wound dew (blood),
Leaving the enemy to feed the ravens.
But stealing swiftly away with precious wealth
from some monastery bejeweled,
or rich prey.
Then for interminable days . . .
Braving the unforgiving, rhythmic sea—
Too often threatening to send them all to Valhalla.

Tonight—should be like any other night so they
thought.

In the moonlight—the long ships with their shallow draft
ground silently into the stony beach.
But! The Angleterres were waiting.
Time to revenge:
Stolen loved and lost ones,
And stolen wealth,
Immediately bonfires were lit, and soon raging—
Turning blackness into bloody day.
In flickering light—arrows fell like heavy rain
on their wooden shields.
And the maddened assailants were upon these gypsies
of the sea.
Clang of steel on steel and flesh shattered the shrieking air.
But to Olaf it was just one more battle, one more victory.
With his great battle ax whirling—about his fearsome body—
He slashed at head, body and limbs,
Crushing, and slicing all in his way—
But suddenly—slung from some proficient foe
A chain struck and circled his great neck—
Powerless he saw it,
Circling his head . . . tightening . . .
As the ball grew nearer.
Its linear momentum now consumed in constricting his neck.
He had thoughts of his young son battling by his side,
And his fair wife at Gotshead on his peaceful farm.
He could see the maiden Valkyries
Riding, rushing to carry him to Valhalla.
As he fell shaking the ground—
And he could taste their welcoming cup of mead.

Till We Meet Again

(Sinking of the Empress of Ireland- May 29, 1914)

The Empress of Ireland a mighty steamship was she
When she slipped away with silent grace from Quebec City.
The fourteen-hundred aboard showed great camaraderie;
Oblivious to the lurking Death soon to show no pity.

While the Saly Ann played "God Be With You Till We Meet Again,"
Many waved farewell to loved ones for one last time,
Unknowing never again would they hear that beauteous strain;
Then all settled happily to the luxury sublime.

Onward to their fate on the mighty river St. Lawrence;
They sliced through the chilled waters in a cloak of fog;
Still there was naught to portend of evil events;
At one a.m. "Pilot put off at Father Point," said the log.

A sinister mate drew near—the Storsted, a collier;
Three blasts signalled the Empress, "Continuing on course;"
The Collier answered but bore onwards without fear;
Now two blasts "Stopping!" cried the Empress fearing the near force.

'Twas a gentle bump in the black night but with sad event;
Explosion! followed renting the proud Empress nearly in two;
In came deadly water, and to an icy grave she went;
But to the dying minute on the bridge remained the crew.

Seven-hundred souls sucked under with the dying liner,
And only fourteen hell-full minutes to put her to sleep,
To lie on her keel where moon eyed fish and sea worms stir,
To be with one-thousand and fifteen in the silent deep.

The screaming surface revealed a maelstrom of activity,
A struggle of icy terror to achieve bliss or pain,
And seven life boats only to prevent calamity.
But for a fortunate few God was there "Till They Meet Again."

The Hanging

The gray dawn and gallows beckoned.
With leaden feet . . .
he climbed the stairs too steep.
Now too soon,
the rope around his neck,
refusing the hood,
heart pounding as if to burst,
he took one furtive last look—
upwards, at life around:
At clouds now tinged in pink in the azure sky,
that he took for granted in yesteryear;
He heard for one last time
the awakening music of birds in the fresh air,
God's creatures he never loved before;
With shallow breaths he sensed the birth of spring;
And saw his mother's face in happy youthful days,
before he went wrong,
but too late now to return her love.
All these he never missed before,
never felt their joys before.
But he loved them now.
Oh! how he cherished them now.
For brief moments only—
he was engulfed and drowned
in this deep longing.

The Collisions that Shook the World

Written several days after September 11, 2001,
day of the diabolical World Trade Center,
and Pentagon terrorist acts—
another "day that will go down in infamy—"
the day we will never forget.

Walkin, strollin' down Liberty Street.,
'Caffeine an' happiness in my veins—
Great morning to be alive.
Feelin' safe and proud in the shadow of (WTC)
Towers One and Two,
The friendly dinosaurs
Gleaming, shimmering in the sun."

Suddenly the sunny air was filled with screams—
Tower One then Two pierced at their very hearts
by slow . . .
deliberate . . .
two hundred ton jumbo jets,
wings angled,
Loaded with hundreds of innocent souls.
Jets driven by twisted madmen, twisted with hate,
Believing themselves heroes,
Believing God would smile on their vile deeds.
Terrorists creating two giant fireballs;
Images that will live forever in the minds of billions.

This disaster resulting in hurried last words
From the near 3000 missing:
"I love you and hope to see you again. If I don't—
Please have fun in life and live your life the best you can."

Collisions that shook the World—
Awakening a mighty sleeping American giant
And the world to terrorism.
Creating scenes of the trapped—hundreds of meters above
Jumping, to 400 metres below, some holding hands—
Some head first,
Some attempting the impossible—to fly,
Choosing this death to a fiery Hell on Earth.
For the others racing against time in the stairwells,

And firefighters moving upwards with heavy
weight,
It was the last minutes and steps on Earth
for the valiant 343 firefighters and near
3000 victims.
Many heroes emerge in the last minutes—
symbols of American might and spirit.
One man carries a lady in wheel chair down 68
floors.

Four years to build but just seconds to collapse
to rubble.
Two dinosaurs down after 31 years, weakened
by the inferno of aviator fuel,
Shaking Manhattan and the World.
Only their shattered skeletons
And painful reminders for millions remain.
Once the tallest skyscrapers in the World,
One hundred and ten stories of architectural genius
Standing majestic in their splendor.
Two small cities down—
Obliterated from the skyline
And the despair and roar of death in these proud
canyons
Heard for miles around.
The lucky ones racing at ground zero chased . . .
by a gigantic yellow wave
Of debris, pulverized glass and deathly soot—
Disbelief, and anguish in their faces of soot
blood and tears.
Now a ghostly scene—gray soot as if from a
volcano
covering Manhattan thick as soup.
The gloom lit only by surrounding buildings afire
Reveals ghosts of the remaining firemen, police,
and derelict cars,
Leaving over a million tons of rubble ten stories
high,
Equal to a mountain of half a million wrecked cars.
Several monumental pieces of outer wall point—
Ominously to the heavens;
The delicate arches a grim reminder of past
magnificence.
While billions of financial papers drift aimlessly . . .
midst the thick dust—
Sad reminders of this fallen financial Giant of the
World.

Now an army of fifty thousand workers,
With help of 400 energetic eager trained dogs
Search and pray for the thousands of missing
And fallen comrades—
In a gray battlefield of death and destruction
At Ground Zero now called Ground Hero.
Smoke miles high marks the deadly tip of
Manhattan.
Mechanical giants: bulldozers, cranes, gigantic
jaws
Appearing like toys next to the mountain of debris
Eat away a tiny bite at a time.
Occasionally a whistle blows—
The roar, clatter and clang, the fury—suddenly
stops,
To hear perhaps a tapping, a muffled cry.
A worker cries out,

"Is anyone there—Is anyone there."
No! Only silence—
And silence again—
When a body is found.
Workers, tiny robots and over 300 search dogs
probe the debris night and day.
Even the caring dogs somehow know
The urgency, the grave importance of their work.
One and all searching for nuggets of life;
Day and night 24 hour shifts,
digging,
lifting,
cutting,
searching,
sifting,
scrutinizing every small piece for remains and evidence.
Looking for evidence like a few special grains of sand on a beach.
Walking a tight rope of rubble:
steel twisted like pretzels,
furniture,
concrete slabs,
All in impossible array.
Breathing in the dust, asbestos, and the stench of death.
Hoping against hope to use the pneumatic air bags to lift weight off survivors.
Then lying down with the search dogs and companions.
Snatching precious sleep for short hours,
exhausted,
frustrated,
Unable to find the missing 4000.
Saving only 18 from the "pile,"
But hoping, praying to save even one.
The last man out, constable McLouglan trapped under 20 feet of rubble—rescued after 25 hours—
survives after 30 operations.
Sixty other police helpers were not so fortunate.

"Both jobs successful;"
Proof of guilt messages to bin Laden intercepted;
These words clear evidence of the deadly deeds.

Meanwhile on Stratton Island a masked army probes the debris
Once again—
Meticulously, with fine tooth comb, raking, raking, and sifting.
The truth must come out, the truth will come out.

"Are you ready. OK. Let's roll!"
Famous last words from Todd Beamer
On UA flight 93—foiled terrorism flight.
These heroic words a battle cry for retribution.

But freedom reigns, freedom will reign.
After all this is the land of the proud and the free.

One Last Drink, One Last Laugh (The Titanic)

On a bright night—a calm night . . .
a night for all the world to recall,
blessed by billions of white stars,
the 'bergs of ice drew nearer . . .
having drifted like creeping death . . .
slowly . . .
from their Arctic home.
The unsinkable Titanic just four days out
Sailed closer . . .
Slicing through the frigid waters,
Ignoring the warnings—
Confidently approached the trap, the death field
Of innocent 'bergs of ice.
Only heaven knew there would be a deadly meeting.
"Iceberg!" The crow's nest cried in frozen fear
Of this historic berg, large above in the chilling air
But gigantic in the black depths below.
"Reverse engines—hard to starboard!" cried the bridge,
But momentum of this monster was not to be denied—
Turn it would not while in reverse—
Its maiden voyage would have its curse.
For most on board little did they know
It was to be their last drink,
Their last dance, their last kiss
And their last laugh.
The unsinkable had met the immovable;
The floating palace versus the terrible mass;
The one in a thousand ships
Meeting one in a million 'bergs.

"No problem—she'll never sink—
Besides the mystery ship looks nearby." . . .
"Alas! it's promising glow grows dimmer each hour." . . .
"Surely they'll see the rockets lighting the sea and sky."
A beautiful sight in happier days,
But now harbingers of death
As they burst aloft with two thousand prayers.
Brief hours before—the Sunday was joy and laughter,
Now replaced by stark fear and the terrible question—
Why!
The prior prayers of peace and hope,
Now replaced by prayers of frozen fear . . .

From afar and from half-filled boats
The women and children see:
The liner still ablaze with lights;
The historic 'berg still lurking near;
On six decks fifteen-hundred black dots shouting and screaming;
Brave men all left behind;

And a few faithful wives, "Where you go I go too;"
The steerage passengers—the third-class cattle,
Alas! Also no chance for them;
And still on board:
Those still searching in panic for lost family and loved ones;
The designer left behind,
In his tortured mind now he could clearly see
The terrible design fault;
And Captain Smith left behind
To die in shame.
The captain's hurried dash to New York
In his once proud ship had failed.

Some on board were lucky indeed
Falling to instant death
Rather than suffer the torture of the icy grave.
Strains of music, Nearer My God To Thee,
A beautiful but mournful hymn,
From some brave souls—carried in the frosty air
To the lifeboats of dismay
And to lonely icebergs beyond—
Suddenly stopped! leaving only cries of terror.

Then from afar the unbelievable sight:
As if some giant hand beneath the ocean
Had pulled her bow under,
Her stern now rising hundreds of feet in the air,
Prop blades exposed . . .
She hung there . . .
For some last moments . . .
Before cracking in two like an egg shell;
Then slipping nearly vertically in slow motion to her grave . . .
Now all life on board extinguished—
In an eerie roar.
For the hundreds left on board it was their last cold drink
And one last cruel joke.
Now fearful to be overturned and cast into the ice themselves
The survivors not responding to the screams of their men
Dared not return;
Reason over-rode love.
In short painful minutes they heard the moaning die away . . .
Leaving only dark silence.

Ship of dreams,
The unsinkable, she's no more—
Now the ship of lost dreams
Lies two mile below—
Shattered—on the ocean floor.

Dust in the Wind

The cherry blossoms blessed the village
when Saburo and his two brothers rode out slowly— . . .
on their prancing steeds in the still morn— the silence
broken only by the hoof beats in the dust
and the clatter of the harness and armour,
while the new born sun danced on steel plate and helmets.
With tears in her eyes his mother had clad Saburo
in the strong light armour bound with silken cord and steel links,
and the steel helmet and long steel blade of his father
given to him by his lord for prowess in battle.

The few who saw the trio with painted faces
from inside the walls of bamboo and under the roofs of sod—
sensed this mission could only be deadly;
but they knew not of this ride of revenge.
Saburo knew Yoko would be watching—
his mind wandered to her jet black hair and the almond skin
he loved to touch—and he was determined to return to her.
To die was to be born again to a better life
but he loved the mountains and streams
loved the blossoming of springtime,
worshipped the trees and forest paths,
and his love for Yoko was a fire within him.

As they left the village behind now tiny in the rolling hills
and now filled with cart and horse
and the clamour of reluctant workers—
his mind returned to his mother.
He was her choice to avenge
their father's death against the wicked Shikimoku
contrary to his brother's pleas.
For though the youngest and the favourite,
Saburo had always been the most skilful
with bow and arrow, sword and horse,
and with hands so quick he could catch a fly.
When he rode—the horse and he were as one
and when he hunted—the deer and boar were his alone.
In view of his great skill and strength
he walked tall as a champion
and was much feared—and admired—
as a young courageous Samurai warrior.

He could recall the hours of instruction by his
father and could still hear and see the
whistling arrows
that struck fear in the heart
in the battlefield with his father.
Proud was he to be a Samurai as his father,
proud to be faithful to their lord.
But he hated some of the harshness of this life:
the enemy heads on the spears,
the walking of prisoners over the live coals,
and the torture by knife, fire and water.
And hard to understand were some monks
sometimes fighting as Samurais.

And he loathed leaving behind his youth:
his days so carefree in the mountains
with his hawk,
riding fast as the wind on his horse,
while riding—shooting with his ever true
arrows at the kites making them fall.
But ever confident was he of his immense skill.
with bow and arrow, sword and horse,
and with hands so quick he could catch a fly.
Saburo recalled many times this day the sight of
his father
riding out in front of the enemy,
that filled the opposite hill,
and calling out for a challenger.
Magnificent was he on his white steed
with his steel helmet crested with the two
dragons—
when he was answered by Shikimoku the
terrible.
Many had this Samurai tortured and beheaded,
but the laws of chivalry of the Samurai
were not his evil way.
From that day of doom Saburo could still:
hear their clash and clang of their swords
amidst the golden dust that turned blood red;
hear the shriek of his father's loveable steed
that fell also with his master;
see his father in the white cotton shroud in
the gilded coffin;
smell the strong perfume;
and see at the feast of the souls of the dead
the torches, the bonfires, and the fireworks.

High above, Saburo's hawk oblivious to the deadly
clash
to occur—
wheeled and floated—
in the warm currents while following his master
and surveying the shining hills and valley below
where Saburo and his brothers by his side
rode silently . . .
and where also three warriors
approached slowly . . .
beyond the hill
in armour and on proud black steeds.

As the sun fluttered and died—
a warm wind blew over bodies
motionless—
on the hillside littered with five bodies, armour
and five steeds,
some writhing,
some wandering.
Above, the hawk—black against the copper sky
wheeled gracefully and followed faithfully,
in the direction of Saburo's village,
the one lone rider.

As the cherry blossoms must fall and be
trampled . . .
so each Samurai warrior fell one day;
like the cherry blossoms—
their life short and beautiful
like a dream in the night—
and now but dust in the wind.

The Fallen

Too brief they loved
And were beloved;
They sampled the world;
Too fast life unfurled;
Too quick life blossomed;
Too short music strummed;
Too brief hearts drummed.
They joined the fray;
Some enrolled for play;
Some for golden glory;
Some for love of country;
Some for adventure;
And some were not too sure.
But all bent on peace
And the Hun to fleece.
Then blood spilt, bodies rent,
Souls to heaven sent.
We will remember them
Along with Bethlehem;
Though many decades later
Still our emotions stir
For those who carried the torch,
Those who fell at the ramparts
And the survivors that march . . .
Onwards ever in our hearts.

SPIRIT & SPIRITUALITY

Rays of Heaven

There is a magical moment sublime
To happen but once in a short lifetime,
When an athlete, singer, dancer, or musician,
Reaches, then touches heaven, but never again.

For some moments divine, perfection they caught;
After a road too long, God's gift was wrought.
The sacrifice, the iron will, go unseen
And without restraint none of this would have been.

The athlete floating as a deer in flight—
Gliding swiftly with grace, heart and might.
The singer, with golden chords blessing our ears—
Only an angel's choir could bring such tears.

The dancer oblivious to gravity—
Such sheer agility we shall never see.
The musician with glorious instrument
Lifting many souls up to the firmament.

In this perfect time all was calm within;
All was joyful, and completely tuned in;
All was on auto, and energy high;
The years and tears all behind with ecstasy nigh.

We wonder at these actions so pure and complete
Which lift our souls to a world of no defeat.
For these rays of heaven we also dream—
To touch God, and to be much more than we seem.

Adversity Overcome

It's your turn for adversity,
Striking with lightning severity;
A prized possession gone—now unseen;
For too long the sea was serene.
Fate oft'times bitter dice does toss;
Small solace these when the loss
Even shakes faith in the cross.

But, a tranquil ocean never
Made a skilful mariner;
Strong kites rise against the wind;
'Tis good sometimes to be chagrined;

And joy cannot live without trials,
So sing a song of thanks for miles
Of past troubles defeated;
And for calamities avoided and cheated;

Save your sweetest songs of praise
For health, loved ones, and past happy days;
And sing a song of gratitude
For events turned better than viewed;
Then sing a chorus of cheer
For what remains ever dear.

Stumble But Never Crumble

You can stumble and buckle
But never crumble,
Under stress and duress,
No matter how far you fall
Or what to you may befall.
For when they call
Out your name at last roll call—
Hopefully you will recall—
How you had huge heart not small
Throughout it all.

A Piece of Cake

Life's a piece of Cake: C is for Courtesy,
A is for Aid, K is for Kindness,
E is for Empathy for you and for me.
If towards others we show tenderness,

Kind words, kind looks, kind deeds or any Kindness
Makes all close by to freshen into smiles,
For a kind heart is a fountain of gladness
And can shorten the long tedious miles.

There is always time for some Courtesy
For civility or some small consideration
For strangers, friends, and dear ones daily.
Thus life is sweetened beyond imagination.

Next to love the purest passion is Empathy;
Sharing your fellow man's sorrow halves it
And gladdens the soul to give him love and pity,
While sharing his joy happily doubles it.

An ounce of help will feel like a pound of Aid
When a person is tired and down in the world.
And in the end when their last card is played
And long after, your deeds are unfurled.

Therefore let us give each day a piece of Cake
For even an encouraging look or word
Taking but a heartbeat, can make or break,
And glory be—striking the magic chord.

The Unforgiving Battlefield

The Olympians of yesteryear:
The dreamers, the believers, the achievers,
The Appolos, the Amazons,
In their vibrant youth
Living, breathing, thinking as champions
Each and every hour.
For long years the dream but a glimmer—
The hope a distant flicker.
But while others slept—
Mightily they toiled when success seemed dim,
Driven always by a burning desire,
A flame within.
Eager they were to burst forth
As a dam releasing its boundless energy,
With each cell and sinew sharpened and honed to perfection,
With hope ever in their hearts and wings on their heels.
They had worn the leaden coat of tortuous workouts;
Born the scorching lungs;
Felt the heart threatening to escape the chest;
All a thousand times and more,
With Agony visited too many times,
But in the end tapping the secret of eking out the ultimate
From the miraculous body.

From all corners of the globe they came:
From the lands of iceberg and snow,
Lands of torrid heat and palm tree;
Knowing that in some remote spot
There could be an adversary with heart more enlarged,
With a body more adept to pain,
One more determined, who had sacrificed more,
One who has trained harder, smarter,
And three times longer to run one per cent faster.
And knowing there would be freaks above all common men:
Those with an arm like a whip;
Those to soar like an eagle;
Those like a bullet in the air;
Some a blur over the hurdles;
Some with stride devouring the track;
And some with iron limbs and will.
They were the disciples of Speed, Strength and Skill;
They worshipped at the feet of Courage;
Made Pain their reluctant friend, and harnessed Fear;
For this was the only way.
Ever confident they glorified body and mind the Master.

They were Determination, Diligence, and Desire
All in one.
For years running free
With Sacrifice, and Persistence behind them.
And with one thought all:
To hold the chalice on high,
To wear the laurel leaf;
To taste sweet victory—or die!

Decades later a pair of dusty spikes,
A javelin once gleaming in flight to the sun,
Or faded photo, bring back for most
The anguish of victory eluded—like an eel too slippery.
The God's of Chance cast bitter dice for most;
The God's of Fate blessed
A meagre few for sure.
Like ever returning, relentless waves
These pangs wash and awaken the memory
Of those moments of youth,
On the battlefield,
Of the unforgiving track,
And the fickle field,
Where the fate of hundreds was decided
In the blink of an eye, or in a heartbeat.
Then on the winds of chance and fate—
Crashed hopes—blown away.

Again and again:
They feel eager hearts pounding;
See the tens of thousands;
And hear the maddening roar
That lifted them to undiscovered heights
And surprising times,
When victory was in their nostrils
As they plunged for the tape
Strong as a thoroughbred.
And there was glory for all for they were there—
And in their minds they are there still,
Champions one and all.
No! time will not erase
This unforgiving battleground,
Not even for those Olympians who have gone
Where angels fly
To the playground in the sky.

The Legend: Eric Liddell

Legendary Scottish athlete, but born in China to Scottish missionary parents, "the Flying Scotsman," international rugby player, 400 meter winner in 1924 Paris Olympics, hero of "Chariots of Fire "movie, beloved missionary in China from 1925 to 1945, died in a Japanese internment camp in China 1945.

He's running still in the hearts of the Scots,
And over the moors and in the mist.
He's in the warm pubs and on the cobbled streets.
In the Paris Olympics he would no run
His favorite one hundred or a relay on the sacred Sunday,
Still he prevailed
In the fearful four hundred;
The record was his
For God and country,
Speeding like the wind with head back and mouth wide open.
He's still in the souls of the Chinese,
In China where he saved many souls and lives.
In the clang and crush of the packed streets,
And out in the silence of the dusty roads.
He's in the gentle wind,
The soft rain,
And in the rainbow.
His Christian message lives on,
Eric Liddell lives on.

第10回世界ベテランズ陸上競技選手権大会　平成5年10月7日〜17日 宮崎市にて

Runners Prayer

Fear give me your fury;
Let me taste your torment.
Pain give me your worst;
Let me feel your fire.
Unleash these wild steeds
Of Fear and Pain,
So they may be trained and harnessed
To obey my commands.
Let me test my mettle
In the flame of training,
In the heat of battle,
In the cauldron of competition,
And the furnace of the fray,
So I may forge my body, mind, and spirit
Like a sword in the glowing coals,
So they may be harder than steel,
Brilliant, and fearsome.
Then, ever ready for my friendly foes.
This is my prayer oh Lord.

Dig Deep

Dig deep, dig deep
While sluggards sleep,
Relentless toward your dream
Though far away it may seem.
There's a promise to keep
And a glory to reap;
Fame will come in the end
If you'll not break or bend;
Your goal is not for the meek
Your path is not for the weak.
Dig deep, dig deep
While sluggards sleep.

Useless Versus Useful

"Never be entirely idle. But either be reading or writing, or praying or meditating or endeavouring something for the public good." Thomas Kempls early 15th century

Your alter ego will be tempted by Useful and Useless:
Useful offers improving body, mind, spirit and more than this—
All as rewarding and gratifying as an angels kiss.
But Useless tempts with material treats and bodily bliss—
All the while sinking deeper into a despair abyss.
As the days fly by one by one,
Time is lost never to be rerun,
In the end leaving deep regret for deeds undone.

York Minster Cathedral

The 2nd largest Gothic cathedral of Northern Europe.
Building began in 1230 and took 250 years.

The pearly grey "Munster" at York
The most beautiful monster in the universe.
It towers above the city
And dwarfs the houses and the city wall.
Wondrous, yes! glorious, yes!
But step inside The House of God.
Immediately one is
Speechless—taken aback—
By the never ending columns
Reaching to the heavens;
The unbelievable stone work everywhere;
And by the music of the choir and organ,
The ethereal notes intensified by the immensity within,
Touching the soul,
Linking Earth to Heaven,
Bringing tears.
How could man build such a structure unless
Guided by the Hand of God?
The angelic sound continues to stir within me.
To experience the Munster
In all its magnificence—
Is to live it forever.

Magic Carpet Dreams

A man sucked into the whirlpool of Nothingness,
Ambition lacking, without a goal, is a no man,
A nothing, a body without a spirit.
Like a leaky rowboat with but one oar,
He's drifting backwards or standing still,
Never reaching destined shore,
For that missing oar is the missing dream.
It's a pitiful man who has not sired a dream
Or who carries half a volition all their life
While wasting talent in frivolous pursuit.
There's billions like him, the "only ifs" and the "never rans."
But still the chains of indolence can be broken.

Seize! your dream today and grip onto it
As the eagle grips the mountain crag with steely talons.
Now your spirit has wings, and the chance to soar,
As you grasp a dream high and beautiful:
One to make self and others happy,
One to use your God-given talents,
One to tax your utmost strengths,
And one once achieved to leave a legacy for future mankind
Like a bright beacon ever before you.
Hunger for your dream, sear it into your brain.
Think, live, practise your dream each day.
Once seized your flighty dream will lift you on a magic carpet
To giddy heights and many deeds along the way,
Yes, a man caught up in the whirlpool of Nothingness,
The indolent world of screams,
Can escape this vortex like a bird
Springing free—in updraft air
If he has but a prayer—and his magic carpet dreams.

The Port of Opportunity

I come announced not by a golden gong—-
But like a brief soft breeze—
Causing the tinkling of brass chimes.
I come entering not as a dazzling searchlight
into blackness,
But as a crack of light in a dark door,
Hinting at the bright promise within.
I come not with loud feet stalking,
But on padded muffled feet,
For God oft reveals only a hint of me.
Uninvited I visit anyway, anywhere;
I hide in chance acquaintance,
In casual speech, and in accident.
Sadly most will not see me, hear me,
or feel my presence.
Rarely do I linger if unattended
For I exist for but an instant and then
Am gone like the desert wind—
For in my quest there is no rest.
I come in calm or storm, by day or night,
Perhaps in a dream, but I will come.
I answer not to the doubtful and hesitant,
But bring me your dreamers—
Those with a lofty goal
Seared into their very soul.
Bring me those who would become and aspire,
Not those who would acquire and possess.
Bring me your vibrant men and vital women,
Not those in a quagmire of indolence,
Or those bound by the chains of addiction,
Or the warm security of habit;
And not those who would be blown away
By the first gales of adversity.
Bring me those though crushed by defeat
Who rise again, steeled by riveting experience.
Bring me your brave, your hopeful ones,
Those not afraid to throw the dice of life.
Bring me the scholars, the athletes, the musicians,
And the others who have prepared, and prepared.
Bring me those men and women who say I can,
And those who would flee from hell to heaven;
And I will spring them free
Carried on an updraft of dreams,
hope and accomplishment,
To grow golden wings of success
For flight to Godly heights
Of lofty love, or giddy fame.
That golden Port of Opportunity,
That heavenly haven, if it appears to you—
I pray—do not pass it by.

Be Bold Be Strong

Based on some words in a hymn at a church in Myrtle Beach

A dream seared through my brain and there it stirred,
One to tax each sinew if it came true.
It filled my heart with fear 'til I heard:
"Be bold be strong for I am with you."

Each day I chase my dream with eager vim.
Its haunting lament will not let me be.
But I take heart with the voice within:
"Be bold, be strong, for He is with me."

Now I'm running strong and racing tall,
While I dream and scheme of worlds to beat.
He is there to help me conquer all,
And wings He has placed upon my feet.

My pals and I do not stand still and moan.
One and all, a dream we clearly see,
To reach the silver chalice but not alone.
Be bold, be strong, for He's here with me.

Often the road is long and mighty rough,
But sometimes smooth and fast downhill,
Then it's not too hard to be tough.
Be bold, be strong, for I am with you still.

A champion or no, there will be no tear.
My chains I have burst, at last I'm free.
You run not alone, when within you hear:
"Be bold, be strong for He is with me."

Now my dream is near, oh! hear the crowd roar.
I'm floating like a deer, as if meant to be.
Now my spirit takes flight to climb and soar.
Be bold, be strong, for He's here with me.

God In Us

There is a quality the Greeks call 'God in us'
And lately I've seen some who are blessed thus:
A pretty track coach who runs back and forth tirelessly
With cheering words beside her young tots moving speedily.
A young man obsessed with his recently acquired antique machine
Works by day and night at two jobs to pay for his rolling queen.
Or strike the 'red button' of any man or woman of your choice,
Then listen to them talk with fire in their eyes and lightning in their voice;
By chance you've hit in idle talk on their life absorbing topic
Be it watching birds, running, even rocks or fish from the tropic.
Every production of genius must start with this gift;
It gives grit, creates patience, overcomes pain, and spirits lift;
It braves dangers, sustains hope, and makes light of difficulties;
It's the trigger for mustering all the faculties;
It moves mountains, and enables the impossible deed;
With it nothing is so contagious and nothing is outrageous;
With Enthusiasm you're blessed by God indeed.

Running in Satori

Inspired by words in book 'Running Within'
by Dr. Jerry Lynch and Dr. Warren Scott.

Enjoy the body flow,
Gliding—floating—
Effort free.
Enjoy the now;
Enjoy the inner you.
This time is yours alone
To revel in—
As you breathe in—
The beauty all around.
Let your senses sing,
Let your feelings ring,
Feel the hymn within,
Feel the peace within.
Body, mind, and spirit,
All in harmony;
That's what it's all about.
Let your body shout
It's silent vitality,
Let the mind run free in Satori:
Forgetting self,
Going beyond,
Becoming more.
Feel the dynamic meditation
And rejoice in the play,
The mystical dance of life,
Where the journey exceeds the inn.

End of the Trail

Near the end of the trail
In the yawning years
When each sunrise and sunset
Appears more precious—
The Ultimate Race Director
Calls out our number.
Then with life collapsing—
Hopefully we recall
When we did fail or fall:

How we rose up again—
Hardened for the fray—
Unvanquished;
How we played the Game,
Slaying the beasts of Fear and Pain—
Giving all,
Befriending Confidence, Courage and Spirit,
And making the world a better place
In passing by.

Rap, Rap, Rappin' on Heaven's Gate

Rap, rap, rappin' on Heaven's Door:
Forgivin' other's sins of yore;
Forgettin' their sins forever more;
A conscience clear will peace restore;
Praisin' charity, not more lore;
Stressin' goodness not riches galore;
Havin' gratitude for all in store;
Practicin' Christian ways not war;
Havin' patience with your neighbore;
Givin' back to the World you adore;
Lovin' one and all for your soul to soar.
Keep on rappin' on Heaven's Door.

Knock, knock, knockin' on Heaven's Gate:
Avoid the crooked path, walk the straight;
Love your brother man, know not hate;
Judgement day is a certain date;
All hateful deeds He will berate;
'Tis never too late to change your fate;
Never stop knockin' on Heaven's Gate.